Science and Native American Communities

Science and Native American Communities

Legacies of Pain, Visions of Promise

Edited by Keith James

University of Nebraska Press, Lincoln and London

© 2001 by the University of Nebraska Press
All rights reserved
Manufactured in the United States of America
⊗
Library of Congress Cataloging-in-Publication Data
Science and Native American communities: legacies of pain, visions of promise / edited
by Keith James.
p. cm.
Includes bibliographical references and index.
ISBN 0-8032-2595-4 (cloth: alk. paper)—ISBN 0-8032-7615-X (pbk.: alk. paper)
1. Indians of North America—Education (Higher). 2. Science—Social aspects—
United States. 3. Indians of North America—Economic conditions. 4. Indians of
North America—Ethnic identity. I. James, Keith.
E96.S35 2001
305.807—dc21
00-069098

Contents

Acknowledgments

This book is dedicated to Frank Dukepoo and to Amy and Mikela James-Rogers, who all traveled on to the next world too quickly for those of us they left behind. The conference that led to this book was organized in conjunction with the American Indian Science and Engineering Society and the American Indian Higher Education Consortium. I thank the following individuals for serving on the conference planning board: Steve Byers, Jhon Goes in Center, Chuck McAfee, Clifton Poodry, and Debra Reed. Karla Clark-Golden, Jan Echohawk-Kollar, Jan Iron and the rest of the Northern Colorado Intertribal Pow-wow Association, Ron Hall, and the Colorado State University Conference Services office helped execute the conference. Additional help in developing or executing this project came from Ryan Briggs, Bernard Blackelk Ice, Nimke Lavel, Imogene Manulito, Chris Milda, Leo Nolan, Agnes Piccotte, Calvin Standing Bear, Richard Tallbull, and James Torres. The city of Fort Collins, Colorado, through its Fort Fund, provided some financial support for the conference. The conference and preparation of this book were also supported by a grant from the National Science Foundation (NSF #9602376) to Keith James.

To all of the preceding people, to the chapter authors, and to the readers of this work, I offer the following shortened and somewhat modified version of a traditional Iroquois prayer used to open meetings:

Today we have gathered and we see that the cycles of life continue. We have been given the duty to live in balance and harmony with each other and all living things. So now, we bring our minds together as one as we give greetings and thanks to each other as people.

Now our minds are one.

We are all thankful to our Mother, the Earth, for she gives us all that we need for life. She supports our feet as we walk about upon her. It gives us joy that she continues to care for us as she has from the beginning of time. To our Mother, we send greetings and thanks. To all life we say thanks for the manifest blessing you give us.

Now our minds are one.

We gather our minds to greet and thank the Enlightened Teachers who have come to help throughout the ages. When we forget how to live in harmony, they remind us of the way we were instructed to live as people. With one mind, we send greetings and thanks to those caring teachers.

Now our minds are one.

Keith James

Keith James

1. Fires Need Fuel

Merging Science Education with American Indian Community Needs

We need you to help us understand what the white men are up to. My Grandchildren, be good. Try and make a mark for yourselves. Learn all you can.–Tatanka Iyotanka (Sitting Bull)

Sitting Bull knew whereof he spoke: Indian people still need to learn all they can. Not only so that they can come to understand what whites are up to and help whites understand the impact of their own schemes but also so that Indian individuals and communities can fully reclaim their heritage and control their future. Education among Indians has lagged behind that of almost all other ethnic groups in both the United States and Canada, and education has generally not offered what Indian communities need. For instance, in a survey I did in 1995 of a sample of Canadian First Nations in every province, the failure of education systems to teach the skills Indian communities need was the single most commonly cited problem for community development. As Fred Roe of Gwich'in First Nation in the Northwest Territories stated at a conference on sustainable resource development in Arctic and Subarctic Native lands, there is great community concern about education. There is, he indicated, recognition that skills are needed but also recognition that degrees do not necessarily translate into skills that are effective for Indian communities. Moreover, he lamented that those Indian students who do complete degrees, typically with support from tribal funds, are often lured away from communities by corporations and government agencies interested in the reality, or the sheen, of diversity.

Problems with Indian educational achievement are rooted in a combination of several community-level factors. There are economic roots, such as high unemployment levels, even for educated Indians; roots in the physical conditions of communities, such as poor infrastructure and equipment; socio-cultural roots, such as family and community problems that weigh down many Indian students; and institutional or programmatic roots, such as a history of educational materials and systems that are culturally inappropriate at best and assimilationist at worst.

And yet, each of the community problems is also influenced by poor educational attainment among Indian peoples. Economic problems have their external and historical sources, but they have often been made worse by poor financial and resource management and by the inability of tribes and individuals to capture existing economic opportunities and to initiate enough new ones. Physical issues such as poor infrastructure or mentally and physically damaging pollution also have their external causes, but these problems have also been made worse by failed planning and ineffective gathering and use of resources. Doing those things better requires improving the knowledge and skills of tribal members. It hardly needs to be said that family, social, and cultural problems in Indian communities and schools largely began with the actions of the U.S. and Canadian governments and societies. But again, they have been partly perpetuated and exacerbated by Indians' inability to develop systems and strategies for countering negative external influences and marshaling internal strengths to meet the demands of new times. Finally, as with each of the preceding concerns, institutional and programmatic issues in Indian communities are not limited to the educational sector and will not be solved until Indian people, themselves, create institutions and programs that work for them to replace "Indian-focused" programs from outside that often do not meet community needs.

There are strong links among culture, self-governance, health (broadly defined to include individual, community, and family well-being), economics, and education. Therefore, efforts to upgrade these different facets of Indian life must be pursued together if any are to succeed. Education can strengthen rather than weaken communities, but only if implemented differently.

Let us begin with economic development. It requires jobs, planning skills, entrepreneurial skills, technical skills, and infrastructure. Education can be a source of jobs as well as a source of each type of skill just mentioned. Indian education is too often largely staffed by non-Indians, however, such that educational jobs and the funds that support them fall out of Native hands. For example, one Indian band in Ontario I am familiar with established its own school board and took control of the community schools in 1990. Yet, it still uses all non-Native teachers and has no plans to address this situation in the foreseeable future. Similarly, Myra Alexander, a member of the staff at the Native Americans in Biological Sciences program at Oklahoma State University, was unable to find a single Indian high school biology teacher in the United States. The lack of modeling and cultural and community connectedness that situations like this create has several implications. It hinders development of technical skills and knowledge among Indian students; it limits educational energizing of the entrepreneurial spirit in Indian communities; it hinders coordination of education with community needs, values, and plans; and it limits the tempering of Western science by Native thought and tradition.

High past dropout rates among Indians have created skill deficits. Mainstream approaches to education that focus primarily on children, adolescents, and young adults in formal classroom settings would not yield needed skills for many years even if dropout rates suddenly changed. Yet, mainstream institutions and agencies continue to stress minor tinkerings with the same tired approaches. For instance, a staff member at the National Science Foundation, an agency that is making substantial efforts to upgrade science and technology education around the United States and that has been reasonably supportive of my efforts, rebuked me recently for talking about "technical training" as part of "education" for Indians. According to her, that agency is concerned about education in schools, colleges, and universities but not about training, which she saw as an out-of-school focus on low-level skills. First of all, training does not need to be limited to "low-level" skills. Many mainstream organizations provide frequent training for even their best-educated members because, in a rapidly evolving world, it is necessary to do so. Moreover, training and education are not two completely separate things. Technical training generally rests on competence in basic skills, such that basic education and technical training often must go together. In fact, they can work well together for those who lack both because the immediate practical economic value of training provides motivation for acquiring basic skills that are often otherwise lacking.

Education is necessary for training, and training can inspire educational success; this is true for Indians as well as for others who find abstract, lifeless information incomprehensible. For most Indian peoples, education was traditionally combined with other activities and could be provided by anyone with knowledge rather than only by official teachers. By conceiving of training and education as one and the same, we can see the value of bringing adult and nonadult Indian learners together, in and out of school.

As they learn, adult learners could assist with the teaching of children as well as provide cultural, community, and practical grounding for education. On the other hand, children could energize and aid adult learners, providing seed enthusiasm, basic information in straightforward ways, and constant reminders of community obligations. Some adult learners who are introduced to teaching children in this way may be inspired to continue to do so and, so that they might, to continue their own education. Examples of how technical training can spark broader educational interest and how working with youth can inspire adult education come from Frank J. Quinto, the higher education coordinator for the Colville Confederated Tribes. Frank describes an office technology training program that his tribal government put in place that inspired several tribal government workers to go on to college programs. He also told me he was inspired to pursue his own college education after working with young Indians in Alaska; he explained, "always telling them to get an education made me feel guilty and led me to go get more education for myself." He now holds a master's degree. Achieving similar successes on a broader scale requires reconceiving education and training systems and strategies to include Indian ways, including organizing and managing them in ways that increase cultural and community connectedness now.

Let us turn to health. Indian individuals suffer at higher rates than non-Indians from a variety of health problems, including accidents, diabetes, disability, illness from environmental toxins, infant mortality, suicide, and tuberculosis. Some of these problems can be directly attributed to economics and education: Poorer and less-educated people tend to be exposed to more environmental dangers, to eat less well and otherwise take worse care of themselves, and to have fewer resources in general with which to obtain life's positives and avoid life's negatives. Therefore, improving education and economics would improve health. But, conversely, health is also necessary for educational and economic success.

We can see this clearly when we consider health-damaging water pollution, typically from the actions of outside entities, that is present in many Indian communities. In one community in Ontario, it is nitroglycerin from the military; in another in North Carolina, it is various chemicals from paper production; in a third in British Columbia, it is toxins from used ink that was applied as a fertilizer (!) to up-basin ranches. Beyond their direct impact on human and wildlife health, these pollutants also limit economic activity in the areas of fishing and aquaculture, farming and livestock, and recreation. Control of cleaning up these problems cannot be simply ceded to federal, state, or provincial agencies, which were often parties to creating them and have shown limited commitment to addressing them in the past. Action and holistic solutions require Indian community involvement, which requires Indian technicians and scientists who can do the work.

Reduced familial or community health also restrains educational attainment and economic productivity. Failing families and community fragmentation both hinder individual success and limit community coordination and action. In so many of the Indian communities I've visited and heard about over the years, polarization among traditionalists, neotraditionalists, and modernists; among Christians and non-Christians or among different subsets of each group; among the educated and the uneducated; and among members of different extended families has yielded a strange combination of paralysis on important issues and frantic, fruitless activity focused on capturing limited opportunity and hollow power instead of on expanding opportunity and finding true power. In too many communities, split families, spousal abuse, and other family problems hit children hard. But many communities have begun to take steps to heal themselves; and many groups and individuals have turned back toward the family-focused, yet community obligated, yet individual and free, values of traditional culture.

Issues in Indian education, Indian economics, and Indian health flow out of and impact on self-governance. Weak education, poor economics, and problematic individual and community health make it difficult to find ways out of the trap of external control and ineffective internal leadership as well as to find ways to maximize opportunities and strengths. And, of course, problems with tribal governance make reforming education, promoting economics, and upgrading individual and social health difficult.

Paternalistic, manipulative, and exploitative outside control has shaped existing tribal governance systems. Some (I do not mean to paint all tribal governments with the same brush here; some have done good work in difficult circumstances) hollow and inept tribal governments have transferred external influences and failed to find successful approaches to cultural, health, economic, and educational issues. Successful leadership certainly does not require formal education. One of the most courageous leaders I have met was a chief in British Columbia with less than a high school education. To stop the spreading of reprocessed ink that ran off surrounding land and into his people's territory, he blocked the roads. But then he called in non-Indian experts to analyze the water and find the evidence to show that the contaminants it contained were harmful. So, successful *governance* certainly does require access to people with the technical knowledge and skills needed to protect communities and carry out community projects and plans. To maintain Indian control and keep resources circulating in Indians communities, as many of those skilled people as possible should be Indian.

This is even more true now, with the U.S. and Canadian federal, state, and provincial governments seeking ways to shed costs and attempting to pass on to tribes many programs and systems that typically were created from the outside and that have rarely worked well for Indians. For instance, both the Canadian Ministry of Health and the U.S. Indian Health Service are attempting to transfer some of their operations to bands or consortiums of bands. There are opportunities here for local control, improved health systems and procedures, and jobs. But there are also dangers in the strings that are often attached that limit administrative, operational, and personnel changes after transfer. One group of bands in Ontario, for example, negotiated an agreement to take over a hospital that had been run by the Canadian federal government, but the agreement requires continued employment for the largely non-Native existing employees, demands continued adherence to federal policies and guidelines that are set by boards that lack Indian representation, and fails to guarantee long-term federal financial support. The affected bands could end up with less care at higher costs without increased control. As Fred Plain from Giizhgannde First Nation in Ontario stated, we must be "fully aware of the difference between governing . . . and managing programs that will be turned over to bands by [federal and provincial] 'dismantling.'"

External control and influence has weakened culture, and weakened culture allows and promotes ineffective governance, educational failings, environmental degradation, and community, familial, and individual debility. Re-energizing cultures will help address these issues, and addressing these issues will help re-energize cultures. Indian culture is not a weekend performance; Indian spirituality is not localized to particular times and places or separate from the realities of everyday life. In the old ways, culture and spirituality were in productive activity, in education, in leadership, and in approaches to health; and these were in them. I have dealt with a lot of formally educated Indians and with a lot of uneducated ones. It always surprises me that there are some people on both sides who see education and tradition as incompatible. Perhaps it shouldn't surprise me, since they have often been executed in recent generations in incompatible ways. And yet, like Sitting Bull, the true "practitioners of Indian culture," to use my friend Jhon Goes in Center's phrase, are often those who best recognize the potential value of education for Indian people and communities and the very real link between education and tradition. For Indians, education that is not grounded in tradition cannot succeed.

Many studies have shown that incorporating Indian cultural principles and tribal languages into education increases the likelihood of Indian students' success. Even if some individuals get through standard mainstream education and achieve conventional success, communities cannot thrive on it, and there are no Indians without thriving Indian communities. On the other hand, Indian education can and does in some places contribute to the continuity of tradition. I remember my friend Rik Yellow Bird (who was unfortunately killed in a car accident a couple of years ago just as he was rediscovering his power and role) talking about Canadian government projections for the extinction of the Cree language not long into the twenty-first century. He talked about the value of that projection and like events in motivating his and other Cree communities to work to incorporate more Cree into the schools and to develop other efforts to maintain and strengthen Cree culture. Many non-Cree communities have done similar things and have begun to turn education into a tool for culture rather than against it. Of course, education will alter culture. But then, everything does and nothing does. Indian people and the core of Indian cultures have survived despite the best and worst efforts to destroy them. They have, of course, evolved and will continue to evolve, for life does not stay static. But there is continuity in the change. In my other manifestation, as a research psychologist, I study the "why" and "how" of creativity and innovation. And what I have found is that, at their purest, creativity and innovation flow out of culture and tradition and carry culture and tradition, refreshed, back to themselves.

So, how do we reach this ideal of integration of education and community? It will take multiple efforts in multiple places. Communities should share information and ideas and learn from each other's efforts, and, where necessary or beneficial, projects should be collaborative across communities. The contributors to this book report on some efforts that have been made by individuals and communities to integrate Indian educational initiatives with other issues. They also provide ideas for new strategies and initiatives that could be used to promote such an integration.

The chapters in this volume are based on papers that were presented at a conference held at Colorado State University in June 1997. The theme of the conference was finding ways to integrate Indian community goals, needs, and traditions with mainstream science and science education. I believe that we succeeded in achieving the general goals of the conference, even if some of the specifics ended up wildly different than what we thought we wanted. It turned out that we did not completely know what we needed, but we got it anyway. We were fortunate enough to draw a very keen, very experienced, and very thoughtful group of invited presenters. There were some disagreements about specific issues and about the relative value of specific approaches. But we all learned something and left the meeting with renewed energy, fresh insight, and new ideas for things that we want to try to carry out in the future in our communities, in our work, and in our schools.

This book is divided into five parts (culture, community development, environment, self-governance, and the links among the preceding issues and education). It is my belief that all of the components of Indian communities fit together such that you cannot address any one without considering, or acting on, the others. The places where these issues meet are also where the greatest opportunities occur, just as the most powerful and interesting areas of the world are places where different elements meet. Where water meets land at the river's edge—in swamps, in marshes, and in estuaries—abundant, unusual, and beautiful life forms exist. Where salt water meets fresh water, there is usually an area with a higher than normal concentration of life. Where desert meets altitude, there are greater numbers of living creatures than in either purely desert or purely mountainous areas. Just so, where scientific disciplines meet each other, creative advances often occur, and where science meets culture and spirituality, the most interesting and powerful implications of both occur, at least for many Native people.

Given this integration and these areas of overlap, how do I justify dividing the chapters into groups? Most of the chapters clearly touch on several of the five categories, and some address them all. Nonetheless, employing the five sections is a useful heuristic tool that may help readers begin to organize and comprehend complex relations. Each section of the book opens with an introductory chapter in which I attempt to set the stage for the topic of the section, provide some context to and links among the section chapters, and point the way toward how the focus of that section ties into the foci of the other sections. The book closes with a final chapter of my conclusions and beliefs about the future of the intersection of science and Native American communities.

Part 1

Education

Keith James

2. Education and American Indian Communities

A History of Pain, a Future of Promise?

Many of the needs of Indian communities—such as better health maintenance and health care, improvement to infrastructure, or sustainable use of natural resources—require expertise in science and technology. Therefore, the first section focuses heavily (though not exclusively) on science and technology education, while the remaining sections focus on the application of the skills derived from such an education to Indian community goals and needs.

The subtitle "A History of Pain, a Future of Promise?" encapsulates the broad span of perspectives in this section. Cornel Pewewardy and Lillian Dyck review some of the historical context surrounding contemporary Indian views of formal education (Oscar Kawageley and Reggie Crowshoe in later chapters also have much to say about the historical context of Indian education). Both emphasize the pain that Indian communities and students have experienced, and continue to experience, relative to schooling. From their perspectives, radical reshapings of educational systems and radical broadenings of the generally accepted approaches to science are called for in order to promote Indian student achievement as well as the advancement of both Indian communities and science.

Clifton Poodry and Frank Dukepoo, two founding members of the American Indian Science and Engineering Society, present alternative views that seem (on the surface) more in tune with the perspectives of mainstream educational and scientific establishments. Both emphasize the importance of individual effort and parental and community norms that support educational achievement. Neither supports the idea that Indian people have distinctive brain organization or culturally based patterns of learning and thinking. The latter view directly opposes part of the argument made in Pewewardy's and Dyck's chapters, which is one of the reasons I decided to group these particular authors. Interestingly, too, both Pewewardy and Poodry invoke the concept of myths, though in vastly different ways.

I obviously think that the perspectives of both pairs of authors in this section have merit, otherwise I would not have used their writing in this book or invited them to the conference that preceded it. My own opinions encompass some of both views. I see more merit in incorporating tribal cultural content into science coursework and science practice than does either Dukepoo or Poodry. This puts me closer to Dyck and Pewewardy's camp. I came to that position both from direct experience and because there does seem to be some, albeit limited, support for it in the research literature.

As a research psychologist specializing in both organizational psychology and my own unique version of cognitive psychology, virtually all of my research work is quantitative. This puts me, interestingly, closer to Poodry and Dyck than to either Pewewardy or Dukepoo, the latter having essentially stepped away from research during the last decade or so of his life. I have read most of the studies that have examined the effects of incorporating one or another Indian culture into mainstream educational coursework, and that literature seems to generally indicate some promise to this approach (see also Oscar Kawageley's and James Lujan's chapters on this point). It is, however, a literature limited by too few studies of too poor quality. The same conclusions can be drawn about another body of literature that looks at brain/mind functions and learning styles among Indians (see Jhon Goes in Center's chapter for further discussion). In some ways, this literature has an even weaker and more contradictory set of studies, such that any conclusions drawn from it must be even more tentative than those about infusing culture into mainstream curricula. Both ideas seem to me to be worthy of additional consideration and examination, even if they are not worthy of being the basis of widespread action at the moment.

I certainly also agree, though, with the point that both Dukepoo and Poodry raise about the vast breadth of cultures (as well as acculturation) and cognitive tendencies across Indian individuals and tribes. This complexity has been ignored too often in the past, and ignoring it has contributed to major problems for Indian people. Attempts to broadly generalize conceptual or research conclusions about Indians across tribes, or to generate cultural interventions for Indian education that could be widely applied, are likely to be doomed to failure. It may be possible and necessary, however, to develop *templates* of understanding and intervention that tap some widely relevant, broad tendencies and strategies while also being adaptable to unique individual and tribal characteristics and circumstances. In a later section, Reggie Crowshoe and Ofelia Zepeda outline two promising general techniques for linking specific cultural content to educational coursework. These techniques certainly seem worthy of further systematic development and evaluation.

Cornel Pewewardy's chapter also fits, to some extent, into a particular minority view held at the conference—that Indian people should put their energies mainly into things other than mainstream science and formal science education, both of which are antithetical to Native traditions and to the true sources of Native strength. This position responds to the historical use of education and science to try to break or exploit Indian cultures. In addition, in the United States, Canada, and Mexico, education has historically been associated with physical and sexual abuse and the emotional and cultural battery of Indian people. (I limit myself to North America because I have minimal knowledge of the history of South America and no direct experience there. I have been told by some people, though, that education of Indians in South America, when it has occurred at all, has often served the same distorted ends as it generally has in the past in North America.) Subtler versions of harmful scientific and educational practices are still commonly directed at Indian students, Indian faculty, and Indian communities, as some of the authors in both this section (e.g., Lillian Dyck) and later ones (e.g., Gilbert John) point out.

Nonetheless, most of the contributors *do* still believe in the potential value of science education and scientific knowledge for Indian people. I do not believe, however, that either should be done or has to be done as it is done now. Other approaches might yield much better results not only for Indian students and Indian communities but also for mainstream students and mainstream science.

Pewewardy and Dyck also argue that, in addition to specialized science skills, Indian students and communities need a broader and more integrated perspective than is seen in mainstream science. Many of the chapters in later sections of this book also touch upon various potential benefits of integrating more holistic Indian world-views into science education and scientific practice.

All of the authors in this section raise the issue of how the structure and systems of mainstream educational institutions hinder effective faculty service and integrative scientific research and application to Native communities.

Again, this occurs, in part, because such institutions lack a holistic focus or perspective that would allow different disciplines and different institutional missions to spark off on each other. For instance, evaluation and reward structures emphasize achievements that can be claimed individually rather than through broad collaborations. Evaluation is also specialized and much more top-down than bottom-up or lateral; this system tends to both maintain disciplinary divisions and promote adherence to existing and narrowly focused ideas and approaches. Moreover, the hierarchy of prestige in higher education typically puts community service last; education professionals often are not motivated to engage in it or receive little support (or are even actively discouraged) when they do make substantial efforts to serve communities. These factors not only limit the application of the expertise present in mainstream higher educational institutions to Indian (and non-Indian) communities, but they also create climates that make Indian students, Indian faculty, and Indian staff feel uncomfortable and unwelcome.

None of the preceding discussion is intended to justify watering down educational standards. There is general agreement among contributors in this section that educational rigor needs to be maintained and, in fact, increased in some ways. Indian students, like all others, need to be challenged. When low expectations are communicated, low expectations are likely to be achieved. (Gilbert John, Gerri Shangreaux, Jane Mt. Pleasant, James Lujan, Oscar Kawageley, Ofelia Zepeda, and Reggie Crowshoe also slightly touch upon this issue in their chapters.)

Tied to the issue of expectations are stereotypes, both societal and internalized ones. Dukepoo, Dyck, Poodry, and Pewewardy draw attention to the negative impact on academic achievement of internalized stereotypes among Indians. I have been investigating since graduate school the impact of self-identity conceptions on individual cognitive performance. Beginning in the early 1990s, Claude Steele from Stanford University began to gain attention with a similar line of research showing that situations that activate internalized stereotypes about groups to which one belongs—stereotypes that indicate poor group ability of certain types of tasks—actually decrease the ability to perform those tasks. These relatively new lines of research are beginning to delineate substantial relations among stereotypes, identity structures, and manifest cognitive performance. Further research on how this dynamic plays out among American Indian students is important.

In summary, the chapters in this section converge in some ways and diverge in others, just as do tribes and Native individuals. Each contains interesting and important ideas that are part of a needed dialogue on Indian education, science education, and the intersection of the two. Subsequent sections of this book echo the ideas in this one and elaborate the dialogue into something that begins to reflect the true richness of American Indians' experiences.

Cornel Pewewardy

3. Indigenous Consciousness, Education, and Science

Issues of Perception and Language

I was born in the Kiowa Indian Hospital and raised in Lawton, Oklahoma, just before the civil rights years. Like many of my friends, I recall using paper sacks for my school lunchbox. My brothers and I wore army-issue clothes to school and always shopped for the best clothes at the thrift store. I can also remember making cracker sandwiches at home. I do not ever remember wishing we were rich and famous, though. I knew my parents loved me and my brothers, and they only wanted a better life for us than the one they experienced. Picking up a few quarters and dollars for mowing grass around town, or picking up pop bottles, kept me as rich as I thought I needed to be. I know my brothers felt the same way.

My mother frequently told me, "Cornel, everything depends on how you want to look at what happens in life. It doesn't make any difference what is going on 'out there.' *What makes a difference is how you take it.*" That was my introduction to the importance of perception. Maybe that catch phrase from my mother is the source of a lifelong fascination I have had with the mysterious relationship between myths and truths. Children tend to have trouble separating myths from truths. This is of no real concern unless we carry it forward into adulthood and cling to myths in the arena of real living. This does seem to happen to many of us: We accept myths as facts, and before we know it, we have been sold a bill of goods that leads us down a worthless, frustrating dead-end road.

Like many American Indian children of my generation, my fantasy world centered on AM radio, sports (mostly NFL football), and, of course, Saturday matinees at the downtown movie theater. My comic book collection helped me pretend I was a superhero. I pretended my father did not have to go off to training in the U.S. Army and later that he did not have to go off to yet another Comanche Business Committee meeting. I pretended that my mother and father got along well with their respective tribes. I pretended that my mother did not have to go to school at night and that my parents did not have financial problems.

When I first began college, I had a good time partying and therefore did not do well academically. Later I buckled down and studied enough to make the honor roll. I marched in the ROTC band, played college baseball, and helped take over the student union to protest that no American Indian studies courses were offered. That was when I traded all my childhood myths and fantasies for a commitment to live honestly and seek the truth. I became a teacher.

For more than 20 years now, I have been studying and teaching principles for how to maximize learning among American Indian students and how to help such students become successful human beings. In my current work as an assistant professor teaching multicultural education and American Indian education courses at the University of Kansas, I am in a constant struggle to give voice to our indigenous experiences. I, like many other indigenous people, encounter resistance when I raise my voice to speak about injustice. My espoused platform as a teacher has always been to shatter the myths of cheap success and to teach the eternal truths about what it really takes to make the most out of life.

In education, as in other areas of life, power and control are the real issues. Power and control are *the ability to define reality and to get other people to respond to your definition as if it were their own*. What people perceive as real and true about the world is largely shaped by those who establish the definitions, interpretations, and constructs that the masses are taught. People's ideas about reality come from researchers, teachers, the media, churches, family, and schools.

Attractive role models gaze down at us from towering billboards and almost disdainfully dangle before our eyes the way to success. Television commercials are carefully designed and expensively produced to help us "realize" we are far less than what we should be. The advent of computers has made possible a new breed of image where reality ceases to be replicated and begins to be simulated. Can we count on these lovely images to deliver when the chips are down? The chances are that they will not.

How does this relate to American Indians? The American Indian community is under siege by imagemakers. American Indians do not have control over the production of images about themselves in society. Ugly and negative images such as Indian mascots, team nicknames, and the "tomahawk chop" continue to exist. And when events such as the Los Angeles riots, Howard Beach, church burnings, hunting/fishing/gaming protests, and Indian mascot demonstrations are brought before the general public, Indians do not have equal access to the media to tell their side of the story.

Here is a specific example of the power of image: The data continue to indicate that the majority of deaths among American Indians are related to drug and alcohol abuse. Is this surprising when alcohol and tobacco billboards are present in disproportionate numbers in Indian communities as compared to non-Indian communities? Is it surprising given the negative images of ourselves that we are offered by mainstream society? It is naive for us to think that the media has no effect on our, or our children's, choices. Values are by no means developed in a vacuum. Most people, especially young people, are not aware of how much of what they think, of what they consume, and of how they behave are directly and indirectly the result of the media's influence.

Are we conscious of the myths we are presented and of how they differ from who we really are as indigenous people? Colonization is the historical legacy that continues to haunt American Indians. Just look at how our people are portrayed in U.S. history. The wide range of descriptions, from subhuman to superhuman, is amazing. Nonetheless, for most of the history of America, American Indians were mainly portrayed as something less than human. This myth encouraged and supported the execution of the American Indian holocaust, in which 100 million indigenous people died. It continues to reverberate in the minds, lives, and conditions of Indian people and in the minds and culture of non-Indian America.

At the other end of the spectrum of myths about Indians have been fantasies focusing on an idealized Indian, "a noble savage," a superhuman. Whether the myth is about a subhuman or a superhuman creature, the actual histories of the indigenous people are replaced by narratives that justify the ends of the mainstream culture. Where does mythology end and where does history start? Indian people assert a history without written archives, one that is based only on a verbal tradition. History as we are taught in the American school system is almost entirely based upon written documents, which means almost entirely based on the myths of the majority.

Can we turn to science to uproot mainstream myths about American Indians and solve the problems they have created? Or is science, itself, rooted in the very myths we would like it to vanquish? Mythical stories often seem arbitrary, meaningless, absurd. Nevertheless, they appear among all groups of people. The anthropologist Claude Lévi-Strauss always insisted that a myth can be understood only by reference to other myths, never by a scientific formula. This is so, he claimed, because every myth is driven by some obsessive need to resolve a paradox in a society or culture that *cannot be logically resolved.* Paradoxes are to Lévi-Strauss what whales were to Captain Ahab. Paradoxes are to American Indian people what Indian princesses are to young Indian girls. Paradoxes are to American sports what Indian mascots are to sports teams. Paradoxes are to American Indian people what Pocahontas is to the Hollywood-created images of the ideal American Indian female beauty. The paradox of the myth that is official American history is that a country founded on the principles of life and liberty took the lives and liberty of so many of its Native people.

Myths and images shape the subconscious. The conscious mind is the source of detailed thought, but the subconscious mind is the source of power. It is a powerhouse of energy with which the individual can be charged, thus enabling us to recover our strength and courage and to keep faith in ourselves. The subconscious mind is beyond space and time. It is fundamentally a powerful sending and receiving station with a universal hookup whereby it can communicate with the physical, mental, psychic, and spiritual worlds of the past, present, and future.

Since the human mind is only part of the universe, the need for myth probably exists because there is order, not chaos, in the universe. If you feel there is chaos in the world, it is really only chaos in your mind, or in your myths.

The subconscious mind always brings to reality the myths that were planted in it. As individuals believe and feel, so they think, so they are. We do not see the world as it is. We see the world as our minds and the myths they have been given make it. Our perception is the lens for how we see the world. Our thinking is the result of our perception. We interpret the world through the lenses of our expectations. The more we interpret and analyze something, the more we move away from the truth of it. Action follows thought—whatever you think will manifest for you. Psychologists, neuroscientists, and theorists believe that once they have mastered the secret of the simplest form of visual awareness, we may be close to understanding a central mystery of human life: how the physical events occurring in our brains while we think and act in the world relate to our subjective sensations—that is, how the brain relates to the mind.

The sociology of knowledge shows us that human reality is socially constructed. As I move from one reality to another, I experience the transition as a kind of shock. This shock is to be understood as caused by the shift in attentiveness that the transition entails. Therefore, for science and technology to benefit Indian people, or for Indian perspectives to benefit science and technology, we have to understand our frames of mind and create a science and technology that fits with them.

Tribal languages are the natural languages of indigenous people—those languages fit how our minds work. In mainstream schools, however, we are taught English first rather than our indigenous languages, and the content of other subjects is made to fit the form of English. This creates learning problems for Indian students. Whereas English is a sequential language (subject-verb-object), many tribal languages are free–word order languages, which reflects the more holistic thinking to which indigenous people are inclined. We are also taught by mainstream institutions and influences to think in terms of blocks and boxes of time (linear thinking), which does not fit our natural way of thinking.

Instead of calling traditional cultures "primitive," we should say that they are "without writing." People who do not use writing rely more on their sensory perceptions and have developed certain mental capacities of observation that many non-Indians have lost. Those are truly decisive contrasts between "primitive" and "civilized" thinking. For many indigenous people, oral language and the "word" are sacred. In the past, one's word was a bond or sacrament. Today, the word has been replaced by treaties and lawyers. In this light, perhaps we will all be better able to see the strengths of indigenous cultures rather than focusing just on their weaknesses.

We want to help Indian students succeed in science and in life, and we want to use science to help Indian communities and individuals succeed. But how do you measure success? Success in America is usually associated with material wealth, education, financial worth, fame, and social status. But I have been trying to illustrate here that the definition of success, like all other definitions, depends on accepting certain myths. In the Indian way, it is not what you *get* that makes you successful but rather what *you are doing with what you have.* Even many non-Indian people eventually find out that all success must be built from the inside out. The happiest people I know do not really compete against or compare themselves to others. Their success comes from doing their best, based on their nature and their ability.

In my research on healing and educating Indian people, I have come to the conclusion that the solution to many of our problems lies in countering the values and ideals of the American way. I feel that in motivating and preparing Indian students to be successful in their lives we must help them to understand and to include their tribal world-views. Myth is a form of language, and the language of mainstream society and science predisposes us to attempt to understand ourselves and our world by superimposing dialects, dichotomies, or dualistic grids upon experiences that they may not fit. We need to reverse the colonization of our minds so that we can think holistically again. We need to rediscover and recreate our own fundamental myths that will integrate the paradoxes of our experiences and our natures. Only then will we be able to link who we are with what science has to offer.   •

Science should not be a privileged field that is limited only to those who accept a particular mythic tradition. If we, as Indian people, are forced to reject our own indigenous knowledge and our ways of thought to participate in science, then we will be that much closer to cultural extinction.

Lillian Dyck

4. A Personal Journey into Science, Feminist Science, and Aboriginal Science

To begin with, I would just like to say a couple of words of thanks to the elders whom I have had the privilege of meeting over the last 3 to 4 years. I first went to speak to an elder by the name of Mrs. Emma Sand, who works at the Saskatchewan Indian Federated College in Saskatoon. She was a tremendous inspiration to me, and one of the things that she taught me was just to be myself and that was enough. In most of the academic communities I have been in, I do not think that I have ever really been myself.

My name is Lillian Eva Dyck. I have been a full professor in the Department of Psychiatry at the University of Saskatchewan for about a year and a half now. I usually call myself a biochemist, but most of my colleagues call themselves neuroscientists. I have worked in the area of how the brain functions throughout my academic career. Gordan is my reserve. That is where my mother was born. North Battleford is the place where I was born. My mother was a Plains Cree woman. She had two sisters and four or five brothers. All three sisters left the reserve. In my mother's time, reserve life was terrible. There was a lot of poverty, and there were a lot of terrible provincial and federal laws that restricted the freedoms of Indian people. Looking back, I think my mother's strategy for getting ahead was to leave the reserve. Both my mother and one of her sisters married Chinese men.

I identify myself as an urban Indian of Plains Cree extraction. In Canada, they call people like me "first generation restored treaty status Indians." There is a registry in Ottawa that lists who is and who is not an Indian according to Canadian law, which, of course, is based on British law. For more than 100 years, the law stated that Indian women who married non-Indian men lost their federal status as Indians. So, for most of my life, I was not considered to legally be an Indian. In 1985, the law that excluded women who married non-Indian men and their descendants from being "status" (i.e., federally recognized) Indians was repealed because it was finally recognized as sexist by the larger Canadian society. So, I applied to have my status restored and was given a treaty card. Unfortunately, I cannot pass that status onto my son. The law has decided that only the first generation can be restored; that part of the law is being challenged but has not been overturned yet.

As a child I visited the reserve, but before my mother died, she gave my brother and me a very strong message: "Don't go back to the reserve." Indian women and men in her generation generally died very early because of the conditions on the reserves. My mother, as a child, had scarlet fever, which damaged her heart. She could easily have been treated, but Indian people in those days could not get much medical care, so she died from complications at a young age. For many years I very rigidly followed my mother's injunction to stay away from the reserve. But my feelings changed in 1981, when I was 36, the age my mother was when she died. Strangely enough, that was also the year I got my doctorate. At that point, I finally asked myself, "Being an Indian person, what is it all about?" and that is when I started my search for my cultural roots. I went back to my community and tried to sort out who I was. It has not been an easy path because I have spent most of my life away from that community. Yet I know I have within me a heritage that is difficult to describe. It is certainly not simply a genetic relation. As I become more familiar with my Cree culture, I realize that it is something to which I have a deep connection. As I become more familiar with who I am as an Indian, I believe I have improved as a person, which has also improved my science.

When I was a child, we moved around from community to community because my dad ran cafes in small towns in Alberta and Saskatchewan. He would open a cafe in one place, go broke, and we would move to the next little community and open another cafe there. When I was in 9th grade, just entering high school, we moved to a small city called Swift Current, and we stayed there so I could attend high school in one place. It turned out to be a good high school with excellent teachers. The vice-principal took an interest in my brother and told him that he was university material, even though he had been put in the room for "slow" students by some teacher or counselor. His encouragement of my brother kind of trickled down to me. Another thing that led me to go on to the university was economic necessity. My father died when I was in 12th grade, which left my brother and me cut off from any family. I realized that if I did not get an education, I would probably be a waitress for the rest of my life, and I had had enough of that already. Because I had good grades and high achievement test scores, I received a number of scholarships that allowed me to attend the University of Saskatchewan.

The university was a big change from high school. The content was much harder and the classes were huge; I felt a tremendous sense of isolation. The literature on recruitment and retention of women, Aboriginals, and other minorities in higher education indicates that people who are different consistently feel isolated. So we cannot just bring in one Indian student, place her or him in among people and systems that he or she does not understand, and hope that she or he survives. There has to be social support to help their academic ability to flourish. That may require recruiting several Aboriginal students or women into a program at the same time so that they can support each other.

For me—coming from within mainstream society, which did not encourage women or minorities to go into science—my involvement in it took a lot of luck and effort. I think I was pushed by the Creator, who I was unaware of at the time. My brother also helped. He wanted to be a chemist and got a master's degree in chemistry. He wanted me and all of his friends to go into science too. I was also blessed by the Creator with a certain amount of natural intelligence, which enabled me to get through the system as an undergraduate and to build a record that allowed me to go on to graduate school.

Way back in 1966, I got a bachelor's degree in chemistry. I went back to school in 1968 to work on a master's degree in biochemistry. Then I spent about 7 years working as a researcher and had a son, who is now almost 24 years old. I soon realized that I was doing the same work as other people in my department, but because they had doctoral degrees they were getting paid a lot more money than I was. I decided that, both for salary purposes and credibility as a researcher, I had to have a doctorate. So in 1977, when my son was 3 years old, I went back to graduate school and got my doctorate in biological psychiatry.

I have had a pretty conventional research career. I have spent most of that time looking at how brain neurotransmitters (chemicals that communicate between different areas of the brain) function. A second area of research that I have been particularly interested in is differences in ALDH (aldehyde dehydrogenase) isoenzymes, because they are involved in the biochemistry of alcoholism. There are several myths about racial differences in drinking and alcoholism, particularly relative to Indian people. Much of what is printed as "research" and believed by the public is not credible. Part of my mission as a scientist that ties in with my identity as an Indian has been to look at the biochemistry of alcoholism and see if I could set some of the myths right. I did that type of research for about 3 to 4 years. Unfortunately, there was not a lot of funding available to support that work, so I have had to put it on the back burner.

Now I work in a research unit with six or seven other colleagues, all of whom are men. We work as a group; these days most research in my field and many other fields requires collaboration. Ten or 15 years ago, when there was more money to support research, Ph.D.'s could work independently, but now there is a real move toward collaborative research. The idea of collaboration has become very popular, but it is not a model that I believe most Western scientists are particularly happy with. I think that most mainstream scientists would prefer the so-called good old days, when people were more independent.

I have spent a great deal of time over the last 2 years working with Canadian women on science and engineering activities, including service work on my campus and science fair judging in the local community. I have also organized conferences on women in science, and I was very pleased that we were able to organize a conference entitled "Women and Other Faces in Science" in Saskatoon in 1998. At that conference we devoted an entire half-day session to Aboriginal science. As a result, I am beginning to feel more integrated as a person and am starting to use all parts of myself in the work that I do.

Saskatoon is now the biggest city in Saskatchewan. Regina is the second biggest city and is also the provincial capital. There are many reserves all over the province. Most people think that all of our First Nations people live in northern Saskatchewan, but that is not true. We are scattered throughout the whole province.

We have a number of programs in Saskatchewan that are very similar to what goes on in the United States. We have science fiction camps at the University of Saskatchewan, to which we invite Aboriginal students from across the province. We have summer science camps that are run by the Federation of Saskatchewan Indian Nations. The Saskatoon Tribal Counsel Urban First Nations division put on our first youth conference, and we are very fortunate to have a Saskatchewan Indian Federated College, which has three campuses across the province. The main campus shares space with the University of Regina, and it has a science department. Most of the Indian students are in the social work and education departments, and, interestingly, most are female. There are exciting plans under way for an

Institute of Aboriginal Science that will involve the Saskatchewan Indian Federated College, the University of Saskatchewan, and the University of Regina. At the University of Saskatchewan a number of Aboriginal faculty members, support staff, and student representatives sit on the Aboriginal Caucus. We have about 1,000 Aboriginal students, which is quite a large number. Most of those students are in education programs, one of which is the teacher education program. In the College of Medicine, we have 9 Aboriginal students, and several more study pharmacy.

The career that I sort of fell into is primarily an academic one. Among people working in the science industry, those who have doctorates are really a minority. The many more who work as technicians, as research assistants, or in applied science positions have only a bachelor's or master's degree. Therefore, in discussing the need to bring more Native people into science, we need to pay attention to the large number of support staff positions and other such positions that are available without a doctorate.

What has my career satisfaction been? Do I want to encourage other Indian people to become scientists? The research itself has been very good and interesting because I have a very inquiring mind. The research has its ups and downs depending on whether or not the data goes as you would like, because as human beings we have strong beliefs about what our data should show. But, generally, I like doing research. The social environment of academia, however, has not been good for me most of the time.

Happily, there are now alternative perspectives coming into university settings. One of them is a feminist science. This can include many things, but one very positive aspect is the recognition that sciences are done in a social context; that is, they are done by people and should be done for people. For Aboriginal communities, that is one of their major goals: for science to serve our communities rather than damage them. Traditional Western scientists tend to think that science is an end in itself and should not worry about serving community needs.

A perspective similar in some ways to feminist science is Aboriginal science. There are several definitions for this term, and I cover just a couple of them here. One definition refers to the study of Aboriginal knowledge about the topics that are covered in mainstream science. For instance, what was known in traditional Indian societies about subjects such as astronomy, cartography, agriculture, or medicine? In Saskatchewan, for example, there has been a great deal of interest recently in traditional plants for use as herbal medicines and other purposes.

Another approach to Aboriginal science is brought out very eloquently in Reggie Crowshoe's chapter in this book. This approach deals with the traditional ways of knowing about things and integrating this knowledge into a bigger picture. It focuses on understanding and developing Native ways of thinking about life, the world, and the universe. That is something that is missing in most universities, which promote only very hierarchical, linear, rational ways of thinking. Any alternative approach tends to be seen as necessarily unscientific and less valuable.

When we look at great scientific discoveries, we almost always find that creativity and inspiration were crucial. To me, inspiration and creativity are not linear and hierarchical. Take, for instance, the story out of chemistry about Kekule, who determined the structure of benzene. Benzene is a six-carbon, unsaturated organic compound; all the carbons are joined in a ring. Kekule struggled greatly trying to figure out that structure. It was not his rational mind that finally figured it out; instead, he had a dream. He dreamed of a snake, a snake that was coiled in a circle, holding its tail in its mouth. From the dream he realized that the structure of benzene was circular, that it was not linear or any of the other possibilities that his logical mind had considered. He had this creative insight that could have come from the Creator; it was, in any case, an inspiration of a different type than what his logical mind had conceived. In Aboriginal science, we would accept intuitive knowledge and look for a holistic world-view that integrates it with logically and rationally derived knowledge. It would also incorporate ways of knowing that are spiritual, which even feminist science leaves out.

For me to even suggest that the spiritual has a role in science is considered by many of my colleagues to be heretical. The standard view is that there is no room for spirit in science. Similarly, the emotional part of science is generally ignored by the mainstream; yet there is a very large emotional component involved. To be a successful scientist, you have to be very competitive. You have to be confident to stand up before other scientists and defend your work and your beliefs. Emotion drives the black-and-white thinking we tend to take on when we are emotionally attached to our work. If you work very hard at something, you want to think that you have the answer and that the guy in his lab over there is wrong. So there really are both good and bad emotional elements to science that we usually do not talk about.

In my own work, I have started trying to integrate the Plains Cree world-view with Western medicine, using the medicine wheel as a framework. Western science seems very well developed in the physical sphere of the wheel. We do a lot of training, we have a lot of equipment, we have a lot of tools—pH meters, mass spectrometers, and so on—that allow us to do a lot of physical manipulation. Western science is also well developed in the second component of the medicine wheel, the mental sphere. There are many scientific facts, theories, and techniques based on well-developed mathematics or ideas. But the last two components of the wheel, the spiritual and the emotional, are weak or missing.

As I become more comfortable with who I am, I feel more grounded in my traditions, and the past desire I had to quit my work in science has subsided. My voice has become stronger, and I am not afraid to say things that I used to be afraid to say in the past. This comfort has given me a type of strength that is different than what I had before. I am more confident about arguing and defending myself. Now that I am learning to listen to my inner spirit, I am also able to argue in different and better ways.

In conclusion, I repeat that we really do need to bring more Aboriginals into science. It is not just an economic issue, nor is it just an equity issue. Rather, Aboriginal students will both better serve our communities and change the way science is done. We must find a way to heal the hurt we have done to Mother Earth and to ourselves; Aboriginal science can lead the way.

Clifton Poodry

5. How to Get What Indian Communities Need from Science

I thought quite a bit about how to approach this chapter, and I decided to forego any autobiographical discussion. I have also decided not to write, at least not directly, about the programs that are under my direction at the National Institute of General Medical Sciences. We are already making some efforts to make them serve Indian communities, and while I am sure that more could be done in that regard, I would like to make the focus of this chapter more general. I thought a lot about the question "What do I have to say that might be of interest to both academics and people from Indian communities?" What I decided to do is share my thoughts about some of the barriers that have made it difficult for me and, I think, for other Indian academics to find a way to merge our academic careers with our efforts to help our communities. I present these barriers not to make excuses but in an effort to stimulate thought about how we can either eliminate them or, at least, find ways to get around them.

I have spent most of my working life as a university researcher or as a university or government-agency administrator. I have always been envious of those people, such as MDs, veterinarians, or teachers, whose chosen professions allow them direct community contact, which mine does not. As a result, finding ways to serve American Indian communities has been an interest and concern of mine for many years. It is, to me, a very important problem, and one that has been around for a long time.

A number of colleagues I have met over the years who began their professional lives not working directly on reservations or with urban Indian communities have reshaped their work to create positive community impacts. For example, early in her career, psychologist Marigold Linton worked with

NSF-sponsored programs for systemic reform in the Southwest that touched several different reservations, and she is now working at the University of Kansas to build joint programs with Haskell Indian University. Frank Dukepoo, who also has a chapter in this book, started his career as a geneticist but then turned his attention mainly to developing the National Native American Honor Society. Fred Begay, a physicist at Los Alamos, is now working as a science advisor to the Navajo tribe. Jack Ridley, now deceased, was a plant physiologist who took his expertise to the Shoshone tribe for a while before going to work for the Bureau of Indian Affairs in Washington DC.

These and a number of other individuals have made important direct and indirect contributions to their communities. They are few in number, however, and Indian community needs for scientific, technical, and educational expertise are great. I am now getting to know a number of younger Indian people who are involved in the sciences or higher education, and hopefully, in time, we will see them become more active in solving some of the difficult problems that Indian communities face. To do so, they will have to, as Frank Dukepoo, Gilbert John, and others describe in this book, fight through many barriers to do their community work.

The first category of barriers I see is the negative voices that come up whenever academics try to get involved in serving Indian communities. Sometimes they come up in the communities, sometimes they come up in the colleges and universities or other institutions where Indian academics work. There are several types of negative voices that make it difficult at times to go forward and find ways to contribute to community issues and needs. These negative voices can stop the conversation—stop any effort at creating a dialogue between the sciences and community service. I will describe three sources of negative voices: community politics, social stereotyping, and preconceptions. These three are often tied together, and they are by no means the only causes of the negativism that impedes efforts by Indian academics to contribute to communities. They seem to me to be common and important sources of negativism, though, and treating them separately makes them easier to examine though I recognize that they are somewhat interconnected.

Indian people know, of course, that one of the causes of negative voices on reservations is tribal and family politics. My own reservation is a small one, with only about 1,200 people. It has a traditional form of government but is dramatically split politically, which seems to be more the norm than the exception on reservations. One of the things I have noticed through the years is that the rift between the so-called traditionalists and the so-called progressives is more often a rift along family lines than along lines based on real tradition; the fights and factions often reflect interfamily jealousies more than anything else. The political infighting at home has been, for me at least, hard to get past, and I believe that this is often true for other Indian academics. Politics is one issue we have to address if we are to gain the benefits of the scientific skills of Indian academics (or any other type of action that could make a real difference in solving Indian community problems, for that matter). We must find a way to deal with nepotism, factionalism, and other sources of political and social barriers to action in Indian communities.

Indian academics or professionals are also often negatively stereotyped by community members; this can dissuade them from even attempting to engage in community service. It is easier to accept and address stereotyping by outsiders than when we Indians stereotype each other. If particular negative stereotypes are applied to everybody with a certain level of education or in a certain profession, they keep people with different life experiences from being able to work together to achieve community goals or to deal with community problems. There are certain Indian people who want, for whatever reason, to polarize different groups, and one way they do this is by focusing on extreme stereotypes. These polarizers put us in opposing camps, making it difficult to even talk to one another, let alone work together.

Stereotyping of Indians by Indians seems to me to be especially likely in education. In some ways, this is part of a more general form of what I think of as "New Age" educational thinking. There are people who make sweeping claims, for example, that American Indians are traditionally "right brained" and mainstream education is "left brained." The implication is that if you have succeeded educationally, you either never thought like an Indian or have been brainwashed by the schools into no longer thinking like an Indian. Even if there were a little bit of truth to the right-brained Indian, left-brained non-Indian concept, to use it as a way to understand complex people and complex problems is nonsense.

Finally, there are some Indian and non-Indian people who claim to know everything about the wants and needs of Indian communities. I think that we should always be skeptical of such claims. What is the problem with people who know it all? The problem is that it is sometimes hard to get past that first, aggressive wave of opinion and belief to get to an analysis, debate, and understanding of the real issues. Only by understanding the real issues can individuals and groups figure out how to address them. The know-it-alls say they already know what the problems are, what causes them, and what answers and solutions are needed. We need to figure out how to get past that approach and to really think about and discuss the issues and potential solutions without being unduly limited by emotion-laden beliefs that are defined and defended as revealed truths.

The second category of barriers, which occurs mainly within academic settings and affects young academics in particular, is the personal and professional cost of volunteering in communities. There really is some risk in spending a lot of time volunteering or otherwise doing activities that take you away from your primary profession. Indian scientists will be most successful professionally if they invest their time in their professional activities. I believe, in fact, that they will make the greatest contribution both to science and to communities over the years if they become really good at, and successful in, their primary profession. I think this is true because credibility is the currency that will take you to the next level of opportunity. If you are a scientist or a professor, such stages as doing well in your profession, getting recognition in that profession, getting tenure, and keeping your job are very important steps. They provide you access to resources and influence over policies that will allow you to have greater effect later in your career. Indian professionals need to be more aware of these issues. While each of us feels a tug to go home and to serve, we have to balance that desire with our overall professional life. We have to realize that in the long run we may be able to better serve our communities if we take the time to build up our professional successes first.

But, of course, the problems and needs in Indian communities are many, and the number of people with high-level training is small. Even early in their careers, Indian academics feel pressure to try to directly contribute to Indian community issues. The cost of volunteering should not be underestimated; I hope that Indian community members will learn to recognize that young Indian scientists may be able to do only limited community work while they are first starting their careers. Those young people who do come back to try to serve their people do so at a personal cost, which should be recognized and celebrated, if not rewarded, by community members and leaders.

A third barrier to the cross-fertilization of academic science and Indian communities is knowing who is who. This is especially a problem from the perspective of community organizations. After all, who do you turn to if you have an issue or project that needs someone with a certain type of training, a certain type of expertise, and who is also Indian or at least has experience in working with Indian communities? Current databases and other sources of information are all very checkered. Over the years several organizations have started various databases, but most of them are either incomplete or proprietary and therefore not widely available. Even in my position with the National Institute of General Medical Sciences, I have not been able to locate names of all the Indian people holding science degrees, even though I know they are out there. This is a problem that might have some simple solutions. A good and easily accessible reference to people who have valuable skills and expertise useful to Indian communities would be a great contribution. Current organizations have not dealt with this problem; maybe some or all of us should try to do so.

Finally, I want to focus directly on one aspect of reforming educational programs for Indians, which is another major topic of this book. The issue I want to address is what I call "The Problem of the N of One." Let me explain. By "N of One" I mean that, in science, to get information on which to base a decision or policy, we carefully consider how many pieces of information (observations of people or things) we need in order to develop a reliable understanding of some issue. An N of 100 or an N of 1,000 may be a large enough sample size to make it likely that our information will be reliable, depending on the particular problem we are studying. Unfortunately, when it comes to Indian education, too often the data set that is used is an N of One. This happens because we are all experts when it comes to Indian education. We have experienced the system firsthand. We know something about the process, something very personal and very deeply felt. This experience makes us inclined to base our approaches to reforming and executing Indian education on an N of One—ourselves.

Let me describe some N of One views of Indian education. First, there are the survivors. Their view tends to be this: "I survived the system. I escaped being weeded out. I learned the game. The system produced me, so it must be okay." Most Indian people in leadership positions are survivors. If they have achieved positions of power, by definition they survived the system. If you talk to a group of Indian or non-Indian college faculty, they will say that the educational system worked well for them. They might be willing to believe that it has gone downhill since they were in school, but they succeeded in the system and became successful professionally using the credentials they received from it, so they generally feel good about it. Similarly, if you talk to high school teachers or school administrators, many are reluctant to change anything. Why are they reluctant to aid or even acquiesce to change? Because for them the system worked and continues to work. Why change it?

You also have the nonsurvivors, or those who at least struggled a great deal even if they graduated. They view the system as a complete failure. Many of them argue that education itself is non-Indian. And, of course, given the history of mental and physical abuse of many Indian children at boarding schools, these negative views are understandable. It is time, however, to shed the extreme post–boarding school angst that leads some to take on a strongly negative view of any and all formal education.

I believe that the greatest hindrance to increasing Indian educational success is that too many of us have bought into a particularly evil myth. The myth is that our abilities are more determined by our genes or by the nature of the system than by our efforts. In the past, if we heard an outsider say that Indian children are inherently less capable than non-Indian children, or that they could only think in a certain way that prevented them from handling certain kinds of information, we would condemn the comment as racist and would oppose it. But some of us say the same thing about ourselves, and we do not respond. How many parents, if a child fails or does poorly in a math class, will say, "You know, Johnny is good in art. He is not that good in math, math isn't his thing"? You can find people saying the same thing about at least some Indian kids for any subject you pick. How can we believe in such a damaging myth that is without factual basis? Research has documented that many Asian parents under similar circumstances would say something like, "Yes, indeed, my son has abilities in art. My son has abilities in these other areas, but he certainly can also do well in mathematics, and if he did not do well it is because he didn't work hard enough." This is quite a different attitude. The more negative, stereotypic, excuse-making attitude is pervasive across North America, and I am afraid it is perhaps more pervasive among Indian people than among other groups.

It is important for us to think about what is real. Let me conclude by saying that our belief in our opinions and those of our friends; our belief in views of the world that are based on what we, personally, have experienced; and our stereotypes about what Indians are like and what the educational system is like are all quite natural. That these views are frequently wrong or at least overly simplistic poses a big and wonderful challenge to those of us who are concerned about Indian education and who want to strengthen Indian communities. The truth is that Indian people and Indian scientists are very diverse, they do not all think alike, and they do not all have the same experiences or cultures. If we can come together and share our different perspectives and synthesize them, we have a better chance of developing a variety of strategies that will actually benefit the full range of Indian people and their goals and needs. To do that, we will have to change some of our ways. We will have to exercise diligence and work hard to listen with open minds to other people's experiences. Only then will we be able to approach education and educational reform, or community and community issues, from an understanding built on more than an N of One. It is clear that some of the barriers are external, but some we bring on ourselves. My hope is that by working together we can assist the next generation of American Indian scholars to achieve success and also to be more effective in serving their own communities.

Frank Dukepoo

6. The Native American Honor Society

Challenging Indian Students to Achieve

I am going to briefly describe a program for Indian students that I run. It is called the National Native American Honor Society. The Honor Society began at exactly 4:00 A.M. on October 4, 1981. I was in Flagstaff sleeping, but the Great Spirit came and shook me and said, "Write these things down: Indian Success, Indian Education, Success, Happiness." I wrote those words on a piece of paper and then kept staring at them and wondering what they meant. Four days later, on a Thursday (four comes up several times in this story), I was sitting at breakfast and I said, "Why not an honor society for Indian people? Why not?" There happened to be an education conference going on in Flagstaff at the time, so I went over and talked my way onto the conference program as a last-minute addition. I raced back to my office and put together some (four) overheads that explained the honor society idea. Only one person showed up for my presentation, one white woman. She listened to my whole talk and afterward came up and patted me on the back with a tear in her eye, saying, "I feel so sorry for you." I said, "Don't." She said, "You seem happy even though I'm the only one who came to your talk." And I said, "Yes, because if I talk about this again next year and there are two people in the audience, that will be a 100% increase. Eventually there will be four, then eight, then many, many more. You have got to keep thinking positively to reach success." That summarizes a major emphasis of the National Native American Honor Society: to get Indian students to think positively about the ability to learn. It turned out that I was right. The number of people who listened to my idea *did* grow from one to two to four to hundreds, and now the National Native American Honor Society is fully under way.

When I started the Honor Society, students were required to maintain a

3.0 grade point average (GPA) for a semester to qualify for membership. An expert in Indian education came to me and said, "Frank, you know what's wrong with your Honor Society? Your standards are too high. Three point zero? That will never work for Indian students, it is just too high for Indian people. Lower it to a 2.0." I nearly pulled the guy right across the table so that I could strangle him, and I am a peaceful Hopi person. I was outraged, and my response was, "What an insult to Indian people. I never want to hear such negative expectations again. Just for that I am going to move the membership requirement up to a 4.0 GPA for at least one semester." You should have heard him and the rest of the so-called experts on Indian education laugh at that. Even many Indians thought I was crazy. They laughed, they scoffed, they ran me out of meetings. "Do not come back with that crazy idea," they would say. But I stuck with it.

We did make a 4.0 GPA the requirement, and gradually over the years we built up the number of members. In 1990, we had 20 students in the society. We had hoped to double that number to 40 or 50 the next year, but we got to 100 instead. In the following years the numbers grew to 200, then 400, then 600, then 1,000, then 1,200, then 1,400, then 1,800. I estimate that we currently have over 2,000 Indian students in the program. They are not getting mediocre grades, not 2.0 averages. No, they are getting *great* grades, straight A's, 4.0 GPAs. In 1997, we probably inducted 600 new members into the society just in the Four Corners area. We hold a banquet for each group of new members, and it is awesome to see so many proud, successful Indian students all in one place.

The National Native American Honor Society is open to students from grade 4 all the way to graduate school. On joining the Honor Society, students get a certificate and a gold eagle pin to wear, and for each additional straight-A semester they get another eagle pin. We have several high school students who have eight or more eagle pins—straight A's all the way through high school. We have been able to motivate some of our early members to continue with their education into college and beyond. For example, one girl has been in the program 5 straight years. She started in middle school; she is in high school now and has had straight A's for 5 consecutive years. The colleges are after her now. But she is not the only one. It is happening, it really is, and I want to share our success with you because some people are still saying that it cannot be done for more than a few unusual Indian students. It is not impossible. It is very much possible if we set high standards and help students live up to them.

We now have eight straight-A families participating in the Honor Society. Mom and dad have been motivated by their children's experience in the program and have gone back to school, and they are getting straight A's just like their kids. Straight-A families, can you imagine that? There are all kinds of interesting things happening out in Indian country, and this is one of them. It is not a story of me and the Honor Society; it is a story of students and communities and how they can get together to achieve things that might have seemed impossible. They set high goals, they believe in themselves, they work hard, and they have an unfaltering and great spirit. Those are the things that make the society work.

Now, the doubters and doomsayers of Indian education always say to me, "Frank, you are just getting the best Indian students in your society, those who would be achieving in school anyway." They are wrong. Many of our members come from dysfunctional families. Some have been labeled "learning disabled." A number come out of special education programs. We have been able to motivate them all to become good students. How do we do that? With a four-prong program. As I mentioned earlier, we start with high expectations and the belief that any student can succeed in school. We also provide what we call "Eagle Force Training," which is a leadership skill program. We teach Indian students how to be leaders, including how to think and communicate effectively. Through high expectations, leadership training, and other means, we promote self-confidence, because that is a big issue for many Indian children. Finally, we incorporate community and spiritual forces into our Honor Society, which makes it very different from honor programs for non-Indians. It is important to our success that we do not just try to create a bunch of smart Indian individuals; rather, we try to create Indians whose goals include helping other Indian people. In doing so, we teach that both achieving our best as individuals and serving our communities are obligations to the Creator.

Our program promotes success in education, in general, but it also emphasizes success in science because, as Keith and several other authors in this book have pointed out, science skills are important to both Indian individuals and Indian communities. Yet many Indian students struggle with science education. A lot of Indian kids believe that they cannot do well in science. Some believe that it is just too hard and that they, personally, do not have enough talent. Others have bought into the myth that Indian people generally lack scientific aptitude because their right brain is too heavy, or some such thing. I hear that all the time.

I said to one student who was very smart but was still having a hard time in science class, "Son, how come you can't do science?" "Well," he replied, "I've got a heavy right brain." I said, "Well let's just test it out. Walk toward me from over there." And, sure enough, as he walked toward me, his head leaned toward the right side. I said to him, "Straighten up. Walk tall and in balance." And, sure enough, when he tried again he could walk with his head held straight. Indian brain imbalance is all baloney, I say. I do not believe in the idea that Indians are more right brained than other people. I believe that Indians traditionally used their whole brain because that's what my uncles taught me. Down in the kiva, that's what they say: You have to think with your whole brain (and your body and your spirit too). In the kiva or in science people should not pull the two hemispheres of their brain apart but should, instead, try to use them together. We should all use everything we have, which is very easy if we just remove all the doubts and fears and limitations that we put on ourselves. We all need to take those "I can't" thoughts and knock the "t" out of them. We need to say, "I can, I can do anything I set my mind to, and I will."

There are a number of other educational myths about Indian students that we could talk about. For example, there is one about the learning styles of Indians. "The trouble is, the Indian is visual" or "Those Indians are auditory." Has anyone ever claimed that Jews, for instance, learn kinesthetically? I have looked into it carefully and found out that Indians are human and that, as such, they all have different learning styles. If you are tired of teaching one way, teach another way, and then another way, and just mix it all up. That is what Indian people have been doing for thousands of years.

Another issue that is controversial but successful in my program is the lack of stress on culture in the classroom. Instead, I try to teach my Indian students good solid genetics so that they can make it into medical school, which they do. Culture is important to Indian students so that they are rooted in their communities and balanced in life. I do not integrate culture into the classroom because information and techniques should be culture free, even if their application often is not. For example, I do not teach Hopi mycosis or Navajo mitosis. Moreover, there are too many tribes, at least at my university, to successfully incorporate culture into my courses. I am a simple Hopi person; I am not qualified to present Navajo culture, Sioux culture, Apache culture, Pima culture, and the many other Indian cultures that are out there. But if it's culture you want, meet me at First Mesa and be sure to bring your cornmeal. I urge Indian people to get involved with their language and culture at home and in their communities. That is where the hard-core culture should be, isn't it? The Honor Society programs try not to mix up culture too much with the information and skills to be covered in a particular class.

There are, however, some cultural elements that we *do* use successfully in the Honor Society. They involve things that I think a lot of people and schools are afraid to touch: educational, personal, and social values. The education bureaucrats always wonder, "Whose values are you going to teach?" My answer is that I will teach my students my values, meaning Indian people's values. We teach general values such as honesty, decency, respect, responsibility, perseverance, discipline, thankfulness, sharing, all those things. But most of the values I just listed are not solely Indian values, are they? They are human values. We find that they work in many different communities. I recently got a call from a lady in Florida who said, "Would you come down and talk to our group?" "Where are you located?" I asked. "Out in the Everglades," she said. We continued talking, and finally I said, "Oh, by the way, what tribe are you?" She said, "Oh no, honey child, we're not Indian down here, we're black. What I heard you say at that conference, we could use some of that too." I have gone to the Bay area to talk to Asian kids; down to L.A. to talk to Hispanic kids; and to the southern states to talk to black kids. The set of values that we teach works for them all. So, while our program is culture free, it *is* value laden. Educational values are what drives the Honor Society, and they really work.

The Honor Society program at the White Mountain Apache Reservation is one example of the success of the program. Back in 1992, we had a big meeting to honor a large number of Indian kids for getting straight A's. I looked through the list of honorees, and I saw only eight Apaches among them. At the meeting, I happened to sit next to Wesley Bonito, an Apache who passed on in 1996. At that meeting, I started joking with Wes. I said, "Wes, I see only eight Apaches on this list of students. I thought you guys were warriors. I thought you guys were tough. Is school too tough for you?" He said, "We're tough, we're warriors." I said, "It doesn't look like it to me from the low number of Apache kids meeting our Honor Society requirements. Where are your classroom warriors?" I was only kidding with him. But he took it to heart and invited me to come to his community at White River to sit down with the tribal leaders, the teachers, and the parents to work on ways of increasing educational success among Apache students. We met and put together some plans and ideas that seem to have been effective. The number of Apache students entering the Honor Society went from 8 in 1992 to 160 by the end of the following year. Those numbers have stayed up too. We had 150 Apache students one year, then 140 the next, and in 1997 we inducted 180 students from White River, Arizona.

In the Honor Society, we have a saying: "Dare to be different." That is what we teach. What does it mean? It means that it does not matter if people laugh at you; you have got to do what you think is right and to make use of your talents. It means that you have to implement your ideas, and to do that you are going to have to stick your neck out and take chances. When you stick your neck out, some people are going to aim for it. But despite them, you should never give up. That is what we say. Never, ever give up.

Dare to be different. How daring are most adults in their lives? I am sure that many have great ideas, but the problem is that most of us sit around and talk about them, and talk, and talk. At some point you have got to implement your ideas. Do not be afraid to try to put your ideas into effect. They have got to be tried. You have got to take a chance for your people. You may have to jeopardize your career, like I did. I was once an associate professor, but I got busted to junior lecturer after I started putting most of my effort into the Honor Society instead of into research. I was deemed to have lost my academic credibility by my department colleagues. Well, I was an Indian long before I was a scientist, and I think that making a difference in the education of Indian young people is much more important than doing the kind of research that a lot of non-Indians can also do. I jeopardized my own career for that view because I believe in it so much. I am not complaining, though. Far from it: I am thankful for all of the trials and tribulations I have experienced. They were needed for the successes to occur.

Three things that helped me through the struggles I endured were my cultural base, my community base, and the spiritual base that we all have as Indian people. I often go back home to First Mesa and talk to my elderly mother about what it is like to have my head on the chopping block. My dad passed away a couple of years ago, but I still have my uncles, my godfather, and my godmothers out there, and I sit down and talk with them all the time too. I am more than half a century old, but I still rely on the support of my family, community, and spiritual leaders. Try to keep in touch with the bases in your life and your work so that, no matter how hard things get, you can always go back home and get revitalized and rejuvenated.

I want to end with this very important message: There are no shortcuts to a good education. There are no shortcuts to getting a degree in science or mathematics or any other kind of degree or skill. There are no shortcuts to anything that is worthwhile. You have just got to get in there and work, work, work. The one thing I tell the kids in the Honor Society over and four times over again is, "Don't give up. Once you start something, finish it. Finish what you start." You think you have a great idea? Stick with it and get going to make it work. You do not want to cheat. You do not want to take shortcuts. Do not learn just the tricks of the trade, learn the trade. What can an individual student or faculty member do to make a difference in his or her community or elsewhere in this complicated world? You can do your best and work with others. You have friends around who can help you and whom you should help. You have family. You have your culture. You have your talent. You can pull all of them together and make something great from the mix. Anything, even remaking a whole community, is easy if you know how to do it and if you are committed to getting it done. Make the commitment and then never, ever give up.

Part 2

Culture

Keith James

7. Culture

The Spirit Beneath the Surface

The issue of finding ways to integrate cultural traditions into educational practice is important to many of the contributors to this book. The three authors
in this section—Oscar Kawageley, Ofelia Zepeda, and Gilbert John—each
address key aspects of this issue. First, they discuss why and how approaches
to science education and scientific practice need to be linked with the unique
traditions and world-views of different Indian communities. Contributors in
this section and the rest of the book also discuss the dislocations that were
created, and often still persist, when non-Indian world-views were imposed
on tribes. Of interest are areas of integration between community culture
and scientific goals that are needed to address problems such as pollution or
diabetes in Indian communities. Several authors provide wonderful examples
of how Indian cultural traditions and mainstream approaches to science or
education can be made to work together in Indian communities rather than
in opposition to each other.

There are many places where the ability of science and science education to
benefit Indian people can be improved. A number of individuals and groups,
including but not limited to the contributors, consider how we can use science
to better serve Indian communities. Many people, Indian and non-Indian
alike, have also concluded that adding an Indian perspective to science and
education would help improve their ability to serve and survive in changing
times.

What is an Indian perspective on science? Is there such a thing, given the
variety of Indian cultures that I, Clifton Poodry, and Frank Dukepoo discussed
earlier? Lillian Dyck argues that certain general Indian perspectives not only
exist but can and should be used to guide some aspects of scientific study

and application. I want to elaborate on some of her ideas here by describing in greater detail the mainstream perspective that currently dominates the sciences. I realize, of course, that many (though, perhaps, a somewhat smaller percentage than 50, 25, or even 10 years ago) mainstream scientists maintain that there is no "perspective" to science, if it implies values or subjectivity. Science, they argue, is value free, except that it values objectivity and problem solving above all else. To this viewpoint, I, the authors in this section, and some authors in other sections of this book reply, "Nonsense." Some of our reasons for that reply are elaborated below.

Culture has been defined in many ways. I define it here as an organized set of tools and techniques for understanding, predicting, and (at least partially) controlling circumstances and events. And what is science? It is an organized set of tools and techniques for understanding, predicting, and (at least partially) controlling circumstances and events. That Indian people have always had a science of sorts can be seen in the fact that many of the past adaptations and modifications of Indian people were done as systematically and inventively as anything derived from Western science. Corn (see Jane Mt. Pleasant's chapter) and rubber, for example, were brought to their existing form by Indian peoples to meet their needs. Natural versions of digitalis were used by tribes to treat heart conditions well before modern medicine isolated, named, and began using the substance.

Let us turn, then, to the idea that science is systematic problem solving. It may well be accurate to say that most of the professional activities of scientists and engineers can be subsumed under this label, but upon consideration this simply points us to other questions: *What* problems are attempted, *why, by what means*, and *why those particular means*?

Subjectivity begins to creep into science when judgment is affected by the choice of problems (basic or applied) selected for attention and action. The problems that scientists and engineers address are generally *not* the universal want of some amorphous general society or those objectively most significant within a particular area. More typically, they reflect the issues that those parts of society that have significant economic and political power desire to have addressed. Not surprisingly, the benefits of addressing those problems typically go to those powerful groups, and the costs typically fall on less powerful social groups. Scientists and engineers, far from being objective in this process, often belong to the elite groups that benefit and do not belong to the groups that pay the costs. Similarly, a substantial body of research indicates that judgments of the relative merit of a particular course of action *do* tend to be significantly and typically unconsciously distorted by the social group memberships and the social statuses of the judges, of those who will benefit, and of those who will bear the burden of costs (see James, 1993, for a review and discussion). Social characteristics such as sex and race/ethnicity are not always the basis of these groups. But, in practice, the costs fall more on minorities, women, and minority women than on others, while decision-making power and benefits typically rest elsewhere.

The Law of Unintended Consequences indicates that new techniques or devices often yield more unintended than intended outcomes. Experience suggests that these unintended consequences frequently have greater, often negative, impacts on our lives than the original use for which a technology was developed (Marcus and Segal, 1999). One reason for the problems related to predicting the implications of technologies, though, is that frequently little attention is given to even attempting to anticipate unintended consequences. Even the overall ratio of costs to benefits from technology often goes unconsidered for reasons related to values and disciplinary training. Even if overall costs and benefits are weighed, typically no consideration is given to whether those benefits and costs accrue fairly or unfairly for different groups.

Another implicit value in science and engineering that affects answers to the question of the means of solving problems is what has been called the "technological fix" mentality. Technology is seen by many as capable of solving anything, and technical virtuosity is admired in and of itself. These values are so strong among many scientists and engineers that problems are often immediately defined in technological terms and technical solutions are sought regardless of the true nature of the issue. A good example could be found in General Motors in the early 1980s, when massive and expensive purchases of relatively early robotic technology were made in an effort to address market-share losses to Japanese competitors. Much of that technology was later junked when General Motors realized (in part by way of joint ventures with Japanese automakers) that the problem of competitiveness was primarily due not to technological deficiencies but to poor organization, supervision, training, and utilization of the company's human workforce. The technological fix can also inhibit detection of unintended consequences. We see this when scientists and engineers become so fixated on the promises of a technology to solve a given problem that they fail to even consider the problems the technology may create.

A third value or norm that shapes the way science is done and technology is used is a strong orientation toward compartmentalization and specialization.

Although there are clear benefits to some specialization, when it is taken to an extreme, things and people suffer. Reductionism and specialization are valued by Western cultures, in general, and by mainstream science, in particular. They do have some worth. For instance, research indicates than when knowledge, skills, and techniques are rapidly shifting (as they are in most scientific and technical disciplines), great pressure for functional specialization occurs because it assists training and continued mastery (Adler & Shenbar, 1990). But excessive functional specialization has also been shown to reduce creativity and the coordination of the multiple types of knowledge and skills that are necessary to address complex issues and goals (Nemeth & Staw, 1989). The enterprise of attempting to understand, predict, and manage the forces and outcomes that science and technology loose clearly is extremely complex and, therefore, should require extensive interspecialty communication and coordination. We need specialists but also generalists and integrative systems and mechanisms. But the skewed values of modern science (and of some societies) and the structures and systems of sciences as professions tend to inhibit integration and coordination. This has two, mutually reinforcing, negative outcomes. Practical problems result because analyses and judgments tend to have very narrow foci regardless of the breadth of the issue or issues at hand, and those whose values tend more toward integration and synthesis are often driven away from scientific and technical fields.

Scientists and engineers are socialized and trained to value objectivity, but there are at least two problems with how this value is generally put into practice. First, the norm of being objective while gathering and evaluating information related to developing scientific understanding of a specific issue or problem is often unnecessarily and destructively extended to mean that the resulting knowledge should be *applied* without regard to consideration of anything other than its scientific or technical accuracy. Second, while few would argue that attempting to consider information objectively is a worthwhile *ideal*, scientists and engineers often invoke this ideal as a talisman to confer a veil of sanctity on their work despite abundant evidence that the human mind, even a scientist's, is inherently subjective in all its operations. To claim that scientists and engineers generally objectively solve the problems of greatest social import is good marketing but can be damaging to both science and society if substantial numbers of scientists accept it unquestioningly.

Some people are inclined to throw up their hands and say that an attempt to be both holistic and specialized, both rigorous and flexible, is impossible or at least so difficult that we should start with something easier. I did not say that achieving these balances will be easy but simply that they are necessary. They can and will be done. When Indian people develop (or relearn or strengthen) effective strategies for gaining these balances, they will model them for others, and as a result, education for all will benefit. Modifying education so that it is more effective for Indian individuals and Indian communities should be beneficial to non-Indian individuals and communities as well.

There is a need to find creative approaches to problems and a need to find innovative approaches to constantly evolving circumstances if individuals or communities are to survive and succeed. Creativity and innovation are primary topics of my own teaching, research, and applied work.

I sometimes have a hard time getting across to my students that creativity and tradition are not two different things. A number of people believe that creativity means throwing away all existing ideas and values and every old technique, technology, and tradition. A mark of being creative, many of my students believe, is a commitment to newness in all forms and on all issues—a valuing of iconoclasm for its own sake. Many scientists and politicians who give high priority to so-called progress also tend to think that it requires discounting community values and norms. Many Indian people disagree with this view of progress, for good reason, since they have borne the costs of such "progress" disproportionately, while any benefits of it have tended to go to others. Their dislike of that view of progress can make them generally resistant to the ideals of creativity and innovation. Creativity and innovation, however, are not at all necessarily opposed to tradition. Creativity often flows out of tradition, out of socially based knowledge, symbols, and values. To be creative, one has to have a strong base of knowledge both within a particular area and in general. A strong grounding in values, cultural symbols, and ceremonies often provides the raw materials, motivation, and rhythms needed for major creative contributions or effective innovations—if it is recognized that they are not museum pieces. Values, cultural content, and behavioral norms develop through distilled experience and adaptation to places, circumstances, and events. Cultures, including the culture of science, must be flexible enough to restructure themselves as the world, circumstances, and events change, while also retaining a core of stability. Otherwise, like any other living entity that fails to adapt, they will not endure.

References

Adler, P. S., & Shenbar, A. (1990). Adapting your technological base: The organizational challenge. *Sloan Management Review, 30,* 25–37.

James, K. (1993). The social context of organizational justice: Cultural, intergroup and structural effects on justice behaviors and perceptions. In R. Cropanzano (Ed.), *Justice in the workplace: Approaching fairness in human resource management* (pp. 21–50). Hillsdale NJ: Erlbaum.

Marcus, A. I., & Segal, H. P. (1999). *Technology in America: A brief history.* New York: Harcourt Brace.

Nemeth, C. J., & Staw, B. M. (1989). The tradeoffs of social control and innovation in groups and organizations. In L. Berkowitz (Ed.), *Advances in experimental social psychology* (vol. 33, pp. 195–230). Palo Alto CA: Annual Reviews, Inc.

Oscar Kawageley

8. Tradition and Education

The World Made Seamless Again

I was born in Bethel, Alaska, and raised there by a grandmother who spoke only the Yup'ik language. I am forever thankful that she refused to send me to a boarding school, where I would have been forced to speak only English and to abandon my Yup'ik culture. Instead, I attended elementary and high school in Bethel and grew up truly bilingual, learning my Yup'ik language during childhood and English at a later time. But I am mainly thankful that she kept me there because I learned the Yup'ik world-view. I think that the cosmology and the ecopsychology of Native people are what defines us. The Yup'ik people are the participants in Yup'ik culture. They learn Yup'ik values, traditions, customs, myths, stories, legends, songs, dances, human and natural models, and above all, the Yup'ik language. Yup'ik culture creates a heliotropic world-view, a heliotropic mind. The Yup'ik language is also critical because it intimately connects one to the ancestors and their thought world. This is a spiritual, emotional, and intellectual connection that helps to shape all thinking and all behavior.

This cultural template allows the Yup'ik person to answer life's questions. If, for instance, I was asked a question, the answer would involve the whole culture. Bits of cloth, places, language, and other symbols would all come together in my mind to help answer that question. I think that this is a beautiful aspect of the Yup'ik mind: every thought and action and symbol is linked to a pattern that makes for a very whole and healthy person. In a unified, heliotropic Native culture, when we seek the answers to questions about the outside world we are able to find solutions that work for the long run.

Just before 1885 a slight northern wind began to blow on my people in the form of the arrival of, first, Russian and, later, English explorers. Soon that slight northern wind became a gale. In 1884 or 1885, when my grandmother was a young lady apprenticed to an *angellquq* (shaman), missionaries came into her village of Mamterilleq ("the place of many smoke houses") and renamed it Bethel. They established a mission and began to tell us that our culture and our sense of the sacred were evil. In their ignorance, they took our beautiful concept of helping spirits, the Tunraq, and redefined them as demons. They took the beautiful name of the chief of the spirits, Tunrangayuq (who is much like Christ in Christianity), and assigned it to the devil.

Then an agent from the federal government came into Bethel and started erecting new forms of government, implementing the welfare system, and compelling Western education. When the educational system was put into place, all of our children received a 12-year sentence to learn a foreign language and a foreign way of life. Yup'ik people were punished for keeping their traditions, a great deal of damage and hurt was done to us, and the gale became a blizzard. During our nearly 100 years of cultural blizzard, there were many things that became obscured so that we could no longer see or fully understand ourselves or our world. Occasionally there would be a break in the storm, and we would be able to see again for a moment, but then the view would become obliterated again.

Though the federal government and the mainstream churches have given up their overt efforts to destroy Yup'ik culture, there is still much confusion because our traditional values are no longer quite as clear for most of our people; new values have been layered over them. We have become people with a lens that is distorted; we have an astigmatism. We are missing some of the links in our culture; our holographic image is no longer complete. While we can see some things clearly, others are translucent, others are opaque. Destructive behavior has followed from cultural destruction. For example, people are killing each other and themselves at a very high rate—double the rate nationwide. I think this is happening because of the confused identities and world-views that we have been given.

What can we as a Native people do to address situations like the one I just described, which is certainly not unique to the Yup'ik? Our traditional culture contains a relevant story that I will tell in a shortened form. Many, many years ago the season for spring arrived, but the winter never came to an end in a particular village. As winter continued and a big blizzard kept going and going and going, the villagers began to run out of food. Finally, one young man decided to take a risk and go out into the blizzard to seek food. He walked and walked for days on end and finally came to a place where the sun was shining and all of the vegetation was green and growing. As he stepped into that place, he turned and looked back and could see his village off in the distance, completely enclosed in the blizzard. An evil shaman had put a spell on it. But the moment the young man looked back from the place in the sun, the spell was broken. Some of our Alaskan Native people are stepping out of the blizzard and looking back. The spell of education as we know it is breaking and we have begun down the road to restoring ourselves to our place in the sun.

The Alaska Rural Systemic Initiative (A-RSI) is helping us achieve our restoration. It is funded by the National Science Foundation and is helping with the process of healing the schisms between our culture and people and the mainstream system that was imposed atop them. Through the A-RSI, we are changing the mathematics and science curriculums to become a reflection of our Yup'ik culture. We as a Yup'ik people have our own science and have crafted our own form of mathematics. As in Western science, there had to be long and patient observations to build knowledge and theories based on distilled experience with events. That knowledge and those theories are handed down to us in our mythology, our stories, and our proverbs. Our math, our science, and the technologies we developed from them grew out of our world-view, developed from our own mind-set.

We study each small piece of the world in which we live. Once we learn about it, though, we look for ways in which it influences people, influences other natural things, and influences the spiritual aspect of the universe. The holistic and spiritual components of our science are big differences from mainstream approaches. In creating knowledge, there also has to be a touch of the person responsible. There is no such thing as objectivity in our world-view; we cannot and would not separate self from the thing that we are studying. The result is that each piece of knowledge is integrated with our complete cultural template, and generating that knowledge is done to help make our cultural template complete.

Our math and our sciences are also tied to a very intimate knowledge of place. For example, our math has a system of quantification, but quantification is of minor importance to Yup'ik mathematics. For instance, in traveling from place to place, it is not nearly enough to know the numeric distance. That would be considered incomplete knowledge. As a Yup'ik, I would also need to know the topography along the way, the sites where the old villages stood, the creeks that had naddle fish, the places where our ancestors camped, and a whole host of other things that are necessary for personal and cultural survival.

Our traditional technology was also certainly tied in with our world-view. We were, for example, able to refine copper and make it into tools for various uses. But my ancestors' thought system, their language system, and their contact with the unseen world yielded uses of copper that, unlike those in mainstream modern society, did not pollute and did not lead to excessive slaughter of other creatures. Our technology was in harmony with all other parts of the world.

We have also received a grant from the Annenberg Foundation to create the Alaska Rural Challenge, which will help us begin to reconstruct the tribal histories of each of the individual Alaskan Native groups. If you look in the history books about Alaska, there is likely to be, at most, only a very short chapter on Alaskan Natives. Usually it is only two to three pages long, and often an Inuk in front of his igloo is used to represent all Alaskan Natives. There are many more Native groups and traditions than just that one. In our project, students and community members from each of those different groups are getting involved in reconstructing their tribal histories. We began with two villages, Carluch on Kodiak island and Umalaska on the Aleutian chain.

Jhon Goes in Center mentions in his chapter the value of mapping traditional places and examining traditional cartographic knowledge, which is something that we are also doing. Our elders share their knowledge with students and communities, and we ask them questions such as what was known in traditional culture about certain environments or what they knew about the theory of relativity even before Western science discovered it. Can you imagine that? I have gone through the mythology and found some things there that reflect the theory of relativity. Our mythologies are powerful teaching tools, and we must remember to make use of them, as did our ancestors.

We are also working on reviving our Alaskan Native languages. We have had bilingual programs for a number of decades, but they do not work. Our Native languages end up getting forced into Western linguistic molds. As with other aspects of our culture, mainstream linguistics tries to tell us that our ways of knowing, our methodologies, and our knowledge are good only if they are translated into Western ways. I always caution our teaching staff and school districts that they must not Westernize our Native ways of knowing. That was done once before and proved to be very destructive both to the education of our people and to other aspects of their lives. We have to change the idea that knowledge and systems that are not from the Western tradition are no good.

This hostile view of other ways of gathering and organizing knowledge has to change if Native education is to succeed.

I believe that Western thought *is* finally moving closer to traditional Native perspectives. The beautiful new mathematics and science of Chaos, for example, include concepts and feelings that approach some of the components of the traditional Yup'ik world-view. In Chaos science and in other topics and approaches, Western science is finally beginning to understand and value the connectedness of the world. There is also some evidence that it is beginning to add feelings to what had been an emotionally barren approach. I think that's great. The old world-view of Western mathematics and science hindered many considerations and contributed to creating many problems. Now Western scientists are closing the gap so fast that they may soon catch up to where they found us 100 years ago.

One example of how we are trying to meld traditional and Western approaches is that our elders talk to students about the construction of the kayak. Students learn why certain parts of the tree are used for the bow and why other parts are used for the stern. They learn how to make the ribs; how to prepare and sew on skins; and how to make a seal oil and spaghnum moss mixture to use as a waterproof on the kayak. It is absolutely necessary that the students learn the Yup'ik technology and terminology connected to kayak construction, but we also challenge them to link this information to Western approaches. They might analyze the chemistry of the sealant, for example, to describe in Western terms why it works.

As you can see, we are beginning to educate our youngsters using our own knowledge systems and teaching strategies. We are also beginning to produce teachers who are well grounded in their own cultural roots, no matter what group they come from. If they are well grounded, they will be stable enough to support the traditional knowledge systems that we are teaching. I think that is one of the most important things that we want to do in the educational system, which is why we call it a *systemic* initiative; there is a need to broadly reconceptualize and revitalize Native knowledge and to integrate it thoroughly with mainstream science. The latter is an absolute must for our own people and for others; we have much to share with them.

Right now with the Alaska Rural Systemic Initiative and the Alaska Rural Challenge we are working with 20 out of the 48 rural school districts in the state. We have come to the conclusion that for the moment we have to limit it to that number of districts because our resources are limited. In addition, not every village is willing to take the risk of doing something new. Therefore, we are focusing on the ones that *are* willing to try something different. As a result of our work with them, hopefully in the near future we will have model villages that will lead the way for others.

Sometimes I wake up in the morning and say, "Why the heck should we teach Western mathematics, sciences, and technology when they seem to be in virtual mutiny against the universe and against life?" Then later on I say, "Well, I think the Europeans and their ideas are here to stay, so let's take advantage of the things they have to offer that are good and not throw everything out because some things have proven bad for us." There are many things from the Western world that we do not want to lose. So I tell myself, "Let's get our young men and women interested in mechanical engineering to think about developing a small solar-powered engine for my kayak and a bed of solar cells for the back of the deck." Then if I want to cross the Bering Sea to reach ice that is several miles away, I can click on a little button to set my automatic pilot, click on another button to start the engine, and sit back as the propeller drives me along powered by the sun. I can take out my steel vacuum bottle, get a cup of coffee, and relax for most of the trip. Then when I get close, I can turn off the solar motor, take out my paddle, and glide to a stop at the best place to land. Whew, that would be a nice melding of traditional and Western technologies. In my traditional kayak I would still be in tune with my world-view. But I could also get some positive value from Western science and technology without making the intensive and damaging use of natural resources that a gasoline engine would require.

Ofelia Zepeda

9. Rebuilding Languages to Revitalize Communities and Cultures

At first I wondered why I was invited to the conference out of which this book developed. In looking at the list of invited people, as far as I could tell I was one of the few who was more a social scientist than a "hard" scientist. The main reason I was interested in participating was because of the focus on the issue of tying together community and education, whether it is education in mathematics, science, technology, or the other disciplines taught at colleges and universities. When I thought about it more, I realized that some of the work I have done at the University of Arizona *is* very applicable to our efforts to intercede to make Indian education, especially in the sciences, serve Indian communities better. For example, authors of a few of the other chapters mention bilingual education for Native students, or linguistics research, or using Native languages to help Indian students learn about science and math. Those are my areas of expertise, and I will address them here in greater detail than the other authors have done.

First, though, I want to say a little bit about my own background. I am a Tohono O'odem from far southern Arizona. My tribe and closely related ones are at the Keelah River and other reservations farther north in Arizona. Another group of Tohono O'odem live even farther south than the Arizona groups, in what is now called Mexico. We were there, though, before the border was.

There are nine in my birth family, and I am the middle child. I went to public school because I lived in a farming community just off the reservation. I was the first in my family to go to high school. I went to junior college after that and then on to a 4-year university. Eventually, others in my family followed me to college, but no one has gone through a graduate degree program as

I have. All of my degrees are in linguistics, and all are from the University of Arizona at Tucson. After getting my Ph.D., I was the administrator of the American Indian Studies Program for a while, before I was hired in the linguistics department as a faculty member. All together, I have been at the University of Arizona for over 20 years now as a student, an administrator, and a faculty member. I do a wide range of teaching and research, primarily related to the Tohono O'odem language.

A number of authors in this book talk about the need for interdisciplinary science education and practice in order to address the needs of Indian people. That is the type of work I have always done. Though I am considered a social scientist on my campus, I have always had a tendency, even as a graduate student, to cross into "hard" science disciplines. Unfortunately, administrators and many faculty at universities tend to try to define disciplines narrowly, and many faculty become intimidated about trying to cross the boundaries of departments and fields. That finally seems to be changing some recently, though.

Linguistics is a field that you cannot narrowly define. It overlaps, of course, with anthropology, sociology, and psychology, the disciplines that study people; language is a people thing. It also overlaps with education, because language and education are so tightly connected that you cannot separate them. There are also subdisciplines, or areas of study within the sciences, that overlap with linguistics. Archeoastronomy is an example. That is where astronomers work with Native people who practice astronomy and study their astronomical techniques, what they have observed, and their beliefs about astronomic events. I have been involved in research with a number of these kinds of projects through the years because I am a Native faculty member with expertise relevant to "ethnoscience" topics. It has been a double-edged sword for me. I have learned quite a number of interesting things about some of these fields. But those ethnoscience projects have taken up a lot of my time, and I am not sure I like the exploitation of indigenous cultures that I have often seen in these projects. Scientists are taking traditional knowledge, the knowledge held in the culture of a people, and making it a product to be dissected and used for the benefit of non-Natives.

One positive cross-disciplinary collaboration I have been involved in with "hard" scientists is in the area of ethnobiology. At first, when one of the biologists on campus asked me to help with this project, I was skeptical. He was looking at how Native people did what he called "classifications," that is, categorizing plants and animals. That is what some biologists do—make classifications of living things by deciding which are so similar in important ways that it makes sense to put them together in a biological category. It was my impression that the O'odem people would never lay things out in little boxes so neatly. I did not think they would label and compartmentalize things so specifically.

But it turns out that there are some people in the tribe who do exactly that. For instance, men who are hunters of large game know the animals they hunt. They study them carefully and organize their knowledge about them in their own ways. To my amazement, a group of elderly traditional hunters were able to label and organize animals very clearly in the O'odem language. They had definitions of different species and described the relationships among the species very precisely. These men, having learned a great deal about the environment by working intimately with it for survival, had developed their own biological science of a sort. It also contained information that they had learned from others through oral tradition and that they had passed on themselves in the same way. Oral tradition has patterns, schemas, and mnemonic devices that help you remember individual things and connect them to each other so that you can use each at the right time as well as present them effectively to others. That is why Native people do a prayer or a song the same way each time. Oral tradition is the way that the older generation learned things, and it is the way that they pass their knowledge on. So it does make sense that traditional knowledge includes categories and stratifications for things in the world; traditional knowledge is a protoscience.

Everything I have done through the years at the University of Arizona has involved trying to better serve the Indian community. One program that I am very proud of is the American Indian Language Development Institute (ALDI). The ALDI was founded by Lucille Watahomigi, who is a Walopai tribal member. Lucille's main philosophy was to use the resources of the universities to validate the knowledge of community people, to organize it so that communities can formally teach it, and to use it to teach other things such as mainstream science.

The ALDI creates an integrated learning situation for educators of Indian students and for Indian community members that focuses on tribal languages. It runs every summer for four weeks. Teachers and teachers' aides who are involved in teaching tribal languages or doing bilingual education come to our institute. Most participants are full-time teachers in tribal schools, Bureau of Indian Affairs schools, or public schools that have a high percentage of Indian students. But we also encourage parents, elders, and tribal leaders to attend so that they become better educated about their language and about what the teachers from their communities are trying to do with it. The community members also help teach the languages to the teachers as well as help plan language programs.

The majority of the people who come to our language institute are Native people. In fact, non-Native people are often quite intimidated when they find they are in a group of mainly Indian people. That makes for some very interesting dynamics that are unusual for a major research institution. In the last few years, we have had at least 100 participants each summer. Most come from the southwestern United States, but lately we have been getting people from Canada, Central America, and even as far away as the Amazon. In 1997 the oldest person enrolled in the ALDI was 75 years old. Some of your typical college undergraduates, 19 and 20 year olds, have also attended. That makes for an interesting generational dynamic in our sessions. That kind of intergenerational teaching can be very exciting and fruitful for all involved.

We offer courses in the areas of bilingual education, language policy, Native American linguistics, Native American literature, and related issues. We also do language research and assist with developing applied language projects for Indian communities. For example, a project that we are very proud of involved using tribal place names and geography as tools to teach Native students at the Peach Springs schools on the Walopai reservation about several aspects of science and the environment. We put the traditional-language geographic place and process names in a computer system that integrates them with scientific information about the biology, geology, or physics of a particular place. This is used in the kindergarten through eighth-grade classes in the Peach Springs school.

Over the years we have also assisted a number of Native communities with developing new systems for writing their languages. Many of the grammar books and dictionaries of tribal languages that exist now were created by non-Native linguists. We help Native communities develop their own grammar books and dictionaries, ones that are accurate, practical, and useful to their needs. We have also been instrumental in getting a number of tribal groups to develop and draft what are called tribal language policies. These are essentially language-use documents that can be fairly comprehensive. They might include statements such as "The tribal language [e.g., O'odem] is the official language of this Indian Nation, and English is the official second language." They frequently include plans for teaching the language and using it in tribal functions so as to strengthen it. The tribal language policies also typically lay out the type of language research the tribe will allow and under what conditions. We see them as important documents because they allow tribes and Native speakers from the communities to think critically about, and plan for the future of, their language. This issue is becoming very critical now because of the loss of so many tribal languages. You can do something to prevent or even reverse language loss, but you have to sit down and think about what you want to do and how to carry it out. So we teach Native language speakers various skills and strategies for how to work with their tribes in implementing language policies and approaches.

We also assist and train people in developing curriculum materials that incorporate tribal languages. Your elementary schoolteacher on the reservation cannot just write to Houghton Mifflin or Norton publishers and say that he or she wants such and such a book in his or her Native language. That does not happen and will never happen because it is not economically feasible to publish a book in each of the many tribal languages. Instead, the teachers and parents in a Native school or community themselves have to create books and other course materials in the Native language if they want students to learn it. We train them in the skills they will need to do that job well. Native language materials in schools on reservations tend to be pretty crude, while curriculum materials in English always have high-quality print and glossy color pictures. As a result, we are teaching people how to design books and use computers and graphics to create polished Native language curriculum materials. With the computers, scanners, and other technological equipment that are now available, we may yet catch up with the gloss and polish of the English-language materials.

I am very proud to have been involved with creating two national laws now on the books: the Native American Languages Act of 1990 and the Native American Languages Act of 1992. A student from our language institute drafted the core of these laws. They came about when California was about to pass its English-only law. Arizona tends to do whatever California does, and we were worried that an English-only law would ban the use of tribal languages in schools, in the activities of tribal governments, and at our institute. So we went to Washington DC to lobby members of the federal government, we called news conferences, and we took other steps to promote our concerns. Grass-roots community people contacted various members of Congress. We held a gathering in Phoenix of Native language practitioners, advocates, activists, and educators to draw media attention to the issue of Native languages. Eventually we succeeded in getting passed the Native American Languages Act of 1990 and later the Native American Languages Act of 1992. Both protect the rights of tribes to use their traditional languages and encourage the preservation of those languages.

The final issue that I want to discuss developed out of our language institute but will operate separately from it. It is an effort to put together a national center that will bring together all information, expertise, technology, and other resources pertaining to the maintenance, promotion, and revitalization of Native American languages. We think that such a center is very important because American Indian languages have long been in decline. Experts say that all American Indian languages in the United States are endangered. An endangered language is simply a language where not enough of the group's children are learning to speak it to keep it alive in the future. Many tribal languages are at that stage now, and some are already extinct. We want to create a Center for Native Language that is friendly to all Native people: to elders, to children, to hard-core researchers, as well as to those people who never finished high school but are often the true tribal language experts. Through the center, all of these people can work together to preserve, rekindle, and understand Native languages.

The ALDI has been very successful in all areas except funding. For 16 years we operated on soft (short-term grant) monies. We did not know from year to year whether we were going to keep our institute, simply because we had no permanent budget. Finally, in 1995, we got a modest permanent budget, which covers only a full-time coordinator, a part-time secretary, and one graduate assistant. Every year we have to go out and find other resources to hire faculty and to recruit and help support our institute's students. So we have succeeded to some extent, but there is still work to be done to make sure that the institute can continue its mission.

This chapter is a very general outline of some of the things that I have been involved with concerning Native American languages. I think that new initiatives of the sort I have described can contribute to the main focus of this book: finding a way to better tie science and mainstream education to Indian communities' goals and needs. I will certainly be happy to contribute to that effort in any way I can.

Gilbert John

10. Trodding the Circle from Indian Community to University Research and Back

When you first get involved in academics and science, it is exciting coming up with ideas, getting grants, teaching, and doing the other things that young professors are expected to do. Right now I am at that point in my career, and I cannot imagine doing anything else. Over the past few years I have gotten to know other Indian faculty members from around the country who have become dissatisfied with their academic careers and feel a calling to pursue other goals. I worry that I may end up feeling the same way in a few years. This dissatisfaction may stem from a conflict that may exist between cultural commitment and scientific commitment. Based on that idea, I would like to discuss the problems faced by Indian people who are pursuing a scientific career or are currently in science. I do not have the solutions to those problems, but I think it is important to expose and consider some of these issues.

Let me begin by telling you about myself. I grew up on a reservation, which made my life different from those of urban Indians. There are not many Western-educated people among my relatives. Instead, I come from a long line of traditional people who have not integrated into Western society, who still largely live as their ancestors did centuries ago. I do not want to go into the specifics of my family history. Instead, I want to cover some issues that many reservation-reared young people, like myself, struggle with as they decide to pursue a scientific career.

Many reservation-reared Indian students struggle with their cultural identity. Of course, all children today face a disorienting world. Life has sped up, and fads and fashions continue to spread wider and change faster. But it may be worse for reservation children. The forces of tradition remain stronger on the reservation. Indian children there still live with the ways of their ancestors around them while also being partly captured by seductive outside influences and pressures. Many struggle to feel complete in the face of such divergent cultural pulls. Finding ways of assisting reservation children with the integration of the modern and the traditional would aid the success and happiness of these children and their families.

With formal education and mass-media exposure, a lot of reservation kids have lost not only the ability to speak their language but also involvement with the ceremonial parts of their culture. They get caught up with the mainstream view of how life should be and fail to realize that the things that happen in their lives can be understood through, and integrated with, traditional beliefs and practices.

Let me give a concrete example. In the Navajo way, there are ceremonies designed to help people deal with each of the major events of life. I have experienced those ceremonies, and the grounding they have given me has helped me tremendously with all aspects of my life. The cycle of ceremonies creates a beautiful system that roots individuals firmly in their history, their identity, and their community. I know that the traditions of many other tribes can have similar effects. Today, though, those traditions are often seen as opposing the demands of modern life. Consequently, reservation children feel pressured to move away from traditions, but those who lack connections to tribal traditions often quickly begin to feel isolated from their communities, families, and identities. They become lost and alone in life and suffer for it.

On the other hand, remaining involved with tradition can create problems for both Indian students and faculty because of the investment of time and energy the traditional system takes. Indian students end up trying to decide how to invest their time and what to believe in; they struggle to figure out how to operate in two systems that often, as they are organized now, conflict with each other. They also often find that, if they follow tradition, it has to remain hidden during their work in mainstream education or mainstream organizations. Teachers, non-Indian students, and even some Indian students fear traditional systems because they do not understand them, and people typically fear things that are strange to them. This is something that many children who grew up on the reservation have to face. They generally do not feel comfortable talking about these conflicts, which makes it hard for them to succeed in their pursuit of an education.

Spiritual or religious issues are also often very difficult for reservation-raised Indian students to deal with. I believe that the Creator gave the Navajos, all other tribes, and all other races the ability to think in spiritual ways. We may never completely understand the spiritual purpose of the universe or, at least, never be able to put it completely into words. But traditional Indian cultures indicate that it is necessary to incorporate the spiritual into our lives if we are to go forward, improve society, and help the children. Awareness of the spiritual component of life is particularly difficult for Indian kids who want to go into the sciences or mathematics; many struggle with mainstream science's tendency to denigrate religion. This may be even more of a problem for reservation-raised students because spiritual practices and a sense of the sacred are stronger on the reservations and end up permeating many aspects of the lives of the children.

We need to find ways to help Indian people balance spiritual traditions with mainstream education and work. It will be difficult because there are few established approaches and frequent opposition when dealing with things that fall between two areas that most people see as incompatible. Those of us who are in charge of programs for Indian education, or who are involved in research that is relevant to Indian communities, or who are trying to apply science to Indian community needs have an obligation to lead the way. We must show both Indians and non-Indians the benefits of balancing both sides: the spiritual and the scientific.

One important way that we can help our students find ways to balance tradition and education is by being consistent in our messages to our young. It is very easy to tell young kids, "This is how you should behave. These are the things you should believe." But if you then go home and close your doors and live a completely different life than what you preach, kids will certainly know the difference. The actions of others certainly shape how children tend to behave. Much of academic success is determined by adult role models: parents, teachers, and leaders. Being a role model is not a nine-to-five job. You cannot simply run off to the casino, or run off to the bar, or talk bad about your boss, or use drugs, or otherwise live contrary to tradition; kids will see what you are doing and think it must be the way to act. You cannot voice support for education but not seek education yourself if you want Indian children to succeed. Nor will you be an effective role model if you claim that science and spirituality can be compatible but then compartmentalize them or largely ignore one or the other in your own life. The consistency and integrity of role models are essential. They can be difficult to achieve and are too often missing in our Indian communities today.

I was fortunate to have very consistent and very strong parents who allowed me to develop balance in my identity and my skills. In turn, that balance has allowed me to develop an inner ability that is difficult to describe but that has allowed me to bridge and integrate science and tradition. I was able to look to my parents, to my dad in particular, as role models for achieving balance between my Navajo identity and my success in the mainstream. Their influence gave me the strength to pull together the pieces of my life into a beautiful whole. My father has little formal education, not even a high school degree. Just the same, he valued education and showed it by seeking knowledge regarding many different things. He is very knowledgeable about many mainstream topics and issues. Yet through consistent involvement over time he also taught me to value my Navajo traditions. He has never changed his ideas or his basic behavior. He lives what we call the "straight path," the good path. He is not perfect, I know that. He has made mistakes in his life but has admitted and corrected them. His example has allowed me to respect both tradition and education and to find my identity in both. He conveys his message, which can anger some, in a matter-of-fact way. I have learned through experience that it is the truth. Overall, he has taught me to respect all people and all religions.

I also had siblings who were role models; I had other relatives who were role models; and there are also people whom I have never met who were and are role models for me. Role models take many forms and can be found in many places. We need to increase the number of successful Indian role models for our children and find ways to make information about these role models more available to our young people. I try to do what I can to be a role model to Indian young people. I try to convey to them that, if they choose to go into science, it will involve some struggles but that there are ways it can be done. It does not require abandoning tradition; instead, they will be more successful if they can find ways to fit science together with tradition. I know it can be done because I have done it, and I try to convince Indian students that it is also possible for them.

We must also recognize, though, that different people have different talents and inclinations, which we have a responsibility to honor. When people ask me how I achieved the success of becoming a professor, I ask them, in turn, how they define success. Success, in my mind, is not necessarily the number of degrees that you have earned. Success is achieving something difficult and has equal value regardless of what you achieve. A youngster who is shy and becomes a good public speaker is a success. A child who develops his or her athletic ability in an area that takes a lot of practice to be good is a success. Those who are not athletes but are strong students and who continue to develop and improve their academic skill are successes. They are all equivalent in my mind; a person can be successful in many ways. Honing a talent, whatever it may be, and working hard is what makes someone a success, which is another message I think we need to consistently communicate and model to Indian students.

Another struggle for Indian people in science is their strong sense of obligation to give back to their community. When I was working on my Ph.D. and early in my professional career, I asked myself, "What, as a scientist, can I do for my community?" It was tough to find an answer at first. I struggled with the question of how I could turn my teaching and my research to the benefit of Indian communities. In my university classes I teach basic microbiology and microbial physiology. As a university researcher I study cytochrome P450 enzymes and their ability to metabolize xenobiotics. Neither of these things has direct community application.

As I thought about it more, I decided that simply my presence in the community is a big contribution. Clifton Poodry also mentions in his chapter that community presence is a basic requirement and can have a tremendous effect. I agree and think my presence in Indian communities and the efforts I make to be visible to Indian students have positive effects.

I have also been fortunate because my current position at Oklahoma State University (OSU) is structured to allow me to give something back to Indian people; my university classes and my scientific research do not consume all of my time. Many other Indian scientists are not as fortunate, which is something we need to work to change at universities and other mainstream institutions. We have to make them aware that Indian people have obligations to their communities, and we need to get them to build time into the positions held by Indian people that allows them to meet these obligations.

I applied for an academic position in my department at OSU not knowing that they had programs targeted toward Native American communities and students. And when I applied, the department did not know I was Native American. Only when I went to interview for the job did they learn that I was Native American, and only then did I learn that they had a program called the Native Americans in Biological Science (NABS).

The NABS program is funded by a Hughes Foundation grant. It involves reaching out to Indian K-12 students to try to interest them in biological science and to motivate them to succeed at it. Its main component is a summer science camp that uses an inquiry-based approach. In this method of teaching, we do not simply say, "Okay kids, this is what we are going to do in the camp.

This is what you are going to learn." Instead, the staff brings a theme, a topical focus to present to the students in the camp, and helps them develop their own ideas regarding it. We bring in speakers and provide guidance, but it is up to the kids to develop a project and carry it out. They have to think of a problem related to the theme for that summer and then come up with the solutions to that problem. They have to select, design, and carry out the experiments that will provide the information they need. It is always a mystery as to how the camp is going to turn out, but somehow, inevitably, these kids manage to gel within the four weeks of camp and come up with very good projects. At the end of camp they have to give a formal presentation regarding their project to parents, tribal leaders, other community members, and scholars. They generally do a beautiful job.

I have been involved with this program for a few years now, and I think it is tremendous. The program helps students develop the inner strength that is necessary for success not only in school but also in life and in their communities. When they develop that strength, it becomes possible to create a bridge between their Indian culture and Western education. I know it has a beneficial effect because the NABS program has been able to collect very good data on past participants. We have followed some of them through elementary school, junior high school, high school, and a few even through college. You talk to any of these individuals and they will tell you that the NABS camps that they participated in have been a tremendous influence on their ability to stay in school and stick with the sciences.

One problem facing programs such as NABS is that they tend to be funded by "soft money," which is a limited-duration federal or foundation grant for a project or program. How to maintain such programs when the grant ends is something many universities struggle with. In the NABS program, we are in the last years of the grant, and we are faced with trying to figure out how to continue the program. This may be an issue that groups of Native and non-Native faculty and institutions could work together to solve. Perhaps we could devise some ways of developing more stable funding for programs that are effective in bringing Indian students into science.

I noted at the beginning of this chapter that I would not have answers to all of the issues I would raise. I am sure that I do not even know all of the questions, let alone all of the answers. But I have put these ideas out into the arena so that we can think about them and begin to develop answers. These are issues that young Indian kids struggle with; even old Indian kids, like myself, struggle with them. I hope all of you are willing to help me try to address them.

Part 3

Economic and Community Development

Keith James

11. Building Futures Together

Community building and the strength of communities are crucial to the effectiveness of education; similarly, educational effectiveness is crucial to community strength and community development. The authors in this section, James Lujan, Dean Howard Smith, Joseph S. Anderson, Gerri Shangreaux, and Ron Jamieson, directly confront different aspects of important connections between scientific and technical skills and the well-being of Indian individuals and Indian communities. They all outline model applied projects that they have undertaken to try to help address one or more community issues. They describe how increased access to scientific skills and advanced technologies is needed to address Indian community concerns and problems such as poor economies, inadequate infrastructure, and above-average rates of many illnesses. Economic development, health improvement, and infrastructural development are each strongly influenced by the availability of engineering, scientific, and technological expertise. Thus, limited levels of such expertise among Indian people contribute to all three problems. The authors in this section also document how, in Indian communities, the difficulties related to economy, health, and infrastructure hinder educational advancement.

Economic Development

The economies of Indian communities are generally poor. Studies of unemployment rates in specific Indian communities or reservations in the 1980s yielded estimates in the 35% to 80% range. Census data from 1990 and recent U.S. Labor Department estimates of Native American unemployment give lower unemployment figures than these (in the 15 to 40% range), though they are still substantially higher than those given for whites. Moreover, the great majority of employed Indians hold low-level jobs that do not contribute to a high quality of life. Most well-paying new jobs in the coming years will require scientific and technological skills. Indian individuals, however, are even more poorly represented in science and technology education and employment than they are in any other type of education or employment. Businesses centered on advanced technologies are likely to be the leading source of new economic development for communities in the future. If Indian communities are to survive and prosper, they, like everyone else, will need to produce advanced technologies and use them in education, in the production of other products or services, and in management of tribal resources.

In their chapter, Dean Howard Smith and Joseph S. Anderson describe a process they use to help Indian communities develop plans for improving their own economies. These plans thoroughly integrate economic development with other major community needs and goals, including those relating to education. Their integrative perspective fits well with the model and argument I present in Chapter 1.

James Lujan outlines how Southwestern Indian Polytechnic Institution (SIPI) was founded out of the belief among the leadership of several tribes that scientific and technological education was key to the economic advancement of Indian communities as well as to other community development goals. Similar beliefs motivated the creation of most other tribal colleges and were one reason that the American Indian Higher Education Consortium, the national umbrella group for tribal colleges, was one of the sponsors of the conference that led to this book. Lujan describes the evolving efforts of SIPI (and, by extension, other tribal colleges) to work with Indian communities and students to promote Indian communities' economies and other aspects of their well-being.

Health

Higher rates of early death and debilitating illness and injury occur among Indian peoples in Canada and the United States than among any other major subpopulation in either country. A dearth of Indian health professionals creates several problems: It contributes to poor access to health care for Indians. It reduces economic opportunity in Indian communities, because health-related fields are major sectors of employment as well as of existing and new business activity. It also reduces Indian control over what ultimately defines them—their genes and their bodily mechanisms. Finally, it limits advancements of scientific information that might be possible from studying the sources of those aspects of health that differ between Indian and non-Indian peoples.

In her chapter, Gerri Shangreaux describes her efforts to help mainstream medical education programs better serve the substantial health care needs of Indian communities. She also discusses her efforts to create new health initiatives that are better suited to the cultural, physical, political, and resource realities of Indian populations than are the approaches that were developed by and for other groups.

American Indian populations have, by definition, some genetic uniqueness relative to other North American residents; but some Indians also experience different environmental conditions and engage in different patterns of behavior than the bulk of the non-Indian population. As Gerri points out, these differences, along with differences in the prevention and treatment programs that Indian people are likely to accept and follow, mean that interventions designed to improve the health of Indians will also need to differ somewhat from those targeted to other groups.

Gerri also argues for increased research on the causes and consequences of Indian health. The factors behind some of the their health problems are somewhat different from the factors for the same problems in other groups. Cardiovascular illnesses, for instance, are more common among American Indians than among all other ethnic groups except African Americans. Yet, the causes of the relatively high rates of cardiovascular illness among American Indians have been the subject of less research than have the causes of the relatively high rates among other groups, such as African Americans. Interestingly, the limited research that has been done indicates that some precursors (e.g., hypertension and cigarette smoking) to cardiovascular illness have different levels and patterns of impact among American Indians than among whites. For instance, hypertension is significantly more common among Indian females than among Indian males; conversely, it is seen much more frequently among white males than among white females (Martinez-Maldonado, 1991). The reasons for this difference across sex-by-race categories are unclear and deserve greater research attention. Increased research on the influences of these differences could help improve understanding of both the causes and the treatment of cardiovascular illness and, consequently, could benefit both Indian and non-Indian peoples.

Young (1994, p. 220) had this to say about the potential general benefits that have been and could be derived from research on health and illness among American Indians: "Native American populations have . . . contributed substantially to . . . knowledge on the etiology and mechanisms of specific diseases. . . . [For example,] much of what endocrinologists know about human diabetes today is derived from studies conducted among the Pima in Arizona." Indian individuals and groups, however, have long been somewhat resistant to studies conducted by outsiders (as indicated, for instance, by low rates of participation in the U.S. census), and this resistance seems to be increasing. Increasing the number of Indian people in health research professions is, therefore, likely to be necessary both to ensure that Indian health issues receive the attention they deserve and to attain the general benefits of understanding the somewhat unique health processes among Indians.

Infrastructure

As with the examination of economic development and health, a closer look at infrastructure issues points to the crucial need for improvements in scientific and technical knowledge and skills among Indians. A better understanding of how to integrate such skills with existing sociocultural systems in Indian communities is also crucial. Poor infrastructure has traditionally made it hard for Indian schools to function well; has made it difficult to attract private businesses to Native communities; has made it difficult for individual and tribal businesses or tribal governments to function effectively and efficiently; and has contributed to poor health and other community problems.

Ron Jamieson observes in his chapter that, although education itself necessitates infrastructure, the educational infrastructure for Indians has been relatively (compared to mainstream Canadian and U.S. societies) poor. Moreover, because the Indian population in both Canada and the United States is skewed toward youth and is growing, the gap between school infrastructure needs and available resources continues to widen every year.

Most Indian reservations (and Alaska Native villages) in Canada and the United States also have very poor infrastructures of other sorts, such as telecommunications and water and waste management (see Chapters 16 and 17). Taking telecommunications as an example, American Indians generally own substantially fewer telephones and computers and have less Internet access than most people in the United States. Many Indian schools either lack Internet access or have only limited, unreliable, slow, and often expensive access. This discrepancy has had negative implications for education, economic development, the provision of basic social services, and the general quality of life. Innovative approaches are sorely needed to bring new resources to Indian communities that can improve infrastructural development and that can address multiple needs at once. Jamieson and Smith and Anderson tell of just such innovative strategies and mechanisms that can help Indian communities advance their development and control their own destinies.

References

Martinez-Maldonado, M. (1991). Hypertension in Hispanics, Asians and Pacific Islanders, and Native Americans. *Circulation, 83*, 1467–1469.

Young, T. K. (1994). *The health of Native Americans: Toward a biocultural epidemiology*. New York: Oxford University Press.

James Lujan

12. Education as a Tool for American Indian Community Development

Needs and Strategies

Let me describe how I came to be who I am, since my experiences have formed my views of education for Indian people. I spent most of my youth in Bureau of Indian Affairs boarding schools. Because my parents were poor, I was sent off to boarding school to learn some of the white man's ways, as well as some discipline, so that I might end up better off economically than were my parents.

Of course, as all who know the history of Indian boarding schools realize, in those days they tried to force Indian students to assimilate. We were not allowed to speak our Native language, and we were not allowed to practice our tribal cultures. Happily, though, I was taken out of school when I was 8 years old and placed in the Kiva society at Taos Pueblo. For a full year and a half, I learned the ways of my people as well as how to live in harmony with nature. I learned where the sacred places are and the sacred ways of doing many things. But I made a solemn oath that I would leave the things that I learned in my community and not expose them to outsiders, because they are sacred to my people.

As a result of my experiences, I see education for Indian people as a continuum. One extreme of that continuum would be purely mainstream knowledge and purely the white man's way of learning. The other extreme would be purely traditional tribal knowledge and purely the traditional Indian way of learning. Most Indians today are somewhat comfortable functioning in both realms, and they need both to have a healthy identity and a successful life. I feel that it is generally best for Indian people, though, to learn cultural things in community settings and to learn mainstream knowledge in school.

In other words, I am not in favor of a great deal of cultural focus during formal education. I oppose it mainly to try to protect Indian identities and tribal knowledge. Some of our own people, and certainly many outsiders, are selling things from our cultures, and the more we bring culture into the schools the more this is likely to happen. We should keep what is ours—our cultural practices, knowledge, values, and languages—to ourselves. We can teach those kinds of things to our children and to each other, but we should not give or sell them to outsiders.

Having said that, I will also argue that it is important to incorporate Indian community goals and issues, as well as general Indian perspectives, into education and science. Doing so will help Indian students balance and unify the different elements of their lives, help Indian communities retain their educated members, and help science progress. I have to admit that even for me, personally, cultural training and mainstream education were not entirely separate. I actually decided to study science as a result of my time in the Kiva society. It was during my education in traditional knowledge that I became fascinated with plants and animals, which led me into the courses I later pursued in formal mainstream education. During my cultural apprenticeship at Taos Pueblo, I studied rocks, springs, tiny animals, and big animals. One of the things I noticed was that when animals get sick they often cure themselves by eating certain types of plants. I wanted to know what those plants did for those animals and how. So from my education in Indian ways, I learned that there were things I wanted to study in school. Even during my college days, I tried to learn science by associating and connecting it with what I had learned in the Indian way. "Transference" you could call it.

I have made it sound easier than it was; I had to go through a lot of ostracism and a lot of ridicule to succeed. I was put down often when I was in boarding school, both by the white teachers for being an Indian and by some of the Indian kids for trying to be a good student. I see that as still being the big issue for Indian education today: helping Indian students learn to manage and integrate both world-views—the Indian one and the non-Indian one. Despite pressures from both sides, I pushed on to eventually obtain a graduate degree in biology. Since then, I have tried to share the knowledge and skills I gained from formal education with Indian students and Indian communities through my work at Southwestern Indian Polytechnic Institute (SIPI).

I need to give a little of the SIPI history in order to explain my work there. In the late 1960s and early 1970s many Indian people were relocated to urban areas by the federal government, and some others went to cities on their own. The outcome was that Indian communities were losing many of their members. Leaders from the Navajo, Pueblo, and Apache tribes were concerned about those losses. So they decided to work together to build an institute of higher education that would help stimulate new economic activity on reservations in the Southwest, as well as train people from those reservations in the skills needed for the jobs generated by that new economic activity.

The school was also intended to help address the tremendous problems that Indian communities faced at the time and largely still face. Take, for example, basic water and land resources. Indian people have always experienced and continue to experience difficulties with maintaining, understanding, and effectively using natural resources. Cities are growing, populations of people and domestic animals are growing, and lifestyles and technologies are changing. All of these things are increasing the demands for water and other natural resources. So efforts by non-Indians to encroach on the natural resources of Indian communities persist, as they have through recorded history. In addition, another type of encroachment is increasing: the pollution that flows into, drifts onto, or intentionally gets dumped on, Indian lands.

We hoped that by establishing an institution of higher education the Indian communities of the Southwest might be better able to retain members, improve their economies, and deal with fundamental issues such as resource management and pollution that threatened their survival. I was involved from the beginning in helping the tribal leaders organize the school. First, we studied the economies of Indian communities in the Southwest, the characteristics of the labor pool, and possible sources for new economic development. We also examined community problems and goals. We then tried to use that information to identify the training programs that would promote the skills and the technologies needed to help Indian communities and Indian individuals survive and succeed. The concept became a reality with the founding of Southwestern Indian Polytechnic Institution (SIPI) in 1971.

In the years since SIPI opened, we have made some progress toward achieving our goals, but not enough. For example, in 1997 we invited representatives from 119 tribal communities in the Southwest to participate in a workshop focused on identifying critical Indian community issues and developing programs to address them. According to this group, the problems of greatest current concern are the same ones that we identified in 1971: economic development; skill development; and managing and protecting water, land, and biological resources.

The majority of workshop participants believed that technical factors would not be as important to solving those problems as would be sociocultural factors and education. They suggested focusing on revitalizing traditions, finding ways of promoting intertribal and intergovernmental cooperation, and improving political and economic conditions. Those things were seen as at least as important as technology or technical education for solving major community problems.

This group of tribal representatives identified several barriers to solving the problems in Indian communities. Those problems included lack of co-operation among tribes and between tribal governments and local, state, and federal government agencies; lack of community awareness and concern; greed; economic dependence on current land use practices; and lack of education.

The last of the barriers just listed points to the sad fact that there are still not enough Indians getting the types of science and technology education that SIPI tries to promote. Another issue identified by the community leaders, though, was that not enough of those who do obtain needed skills come back to work in Indian communities. I hear myself and other Indian leaders say to young people from our communities, "It is important to learn about science, important to learn about engineering, important to learn other skills, so that you can come back and help your people." Well, the truth is that most who do learn about those things do not return to Indian communities.

Just recently the Taos Pueblo tribal leadership asked, "Where are our people who left the community? Let's find out who they are and where they are." After a long effort, we located many in the cities and towns and at different universities and colleges. We called them to a meeting to ask what it would take to get them to come home. Of those we invited, 55% came to the meeting. Most said that they *do* want to return but that much has to change before they can. There needs to be more jobs but also a return to the traditional visions and improved efforts to address modern realities within the framework of the traditional cultures of our people. Many of those who have left say that they still hope to learn things that will help them make a difference if they do return.

What do Indian students think? During the summer months, we bring Indian high school students in from boarding schools, mission schools, public schools, contract schools, and tribal schools. We ask the students in the summer program about the kinds of problems they see in their communities and the things they want to learn. They say that the issues that matter to them are studying nature and the earth; learning about ecological systems; learning about and from past generations; coming to know who they are as Indians; understanding the fit of family, education, culture, and spirituality; and learning about the universe.

Our summer program participants say that it worries them that Indians from agricultural traditions are losing their farming cultures; that traditional values are eroding; that many people seem to be losing connections with the earth. They believe that more and more people take from the earth and from their communities but give little back, and this concerns them. They also worry about the implications of tribal reliance on gaming, about high reservation unemployment rates, about high substance abuse levels, about the breaking of environmental cycles and patterns, and about the danger of tribes losing old ways and valuable knowledge as the generation of elders dies out. They say they want to learn more about helpful plants in school. We do not use many traditional medicinal plants any more, and our young people want to know more about them. They are interested in what makes a healthy diet and how health might be improved through traditional diets. They also want to learn much more about traditional approaches to the environment. This is only a partial list of the kinds of things that the young people in the SIPI summer program are thinking about.

To try to address their interests and concerns, we take them through a problem-based educational program. They begin to learn science and mathematics by trying to tackle real problems that need to be solved using science and math knowledge. They end up accomplishing things and learning at the same time, and this makes them feel proud. The only problem we find as we follow up on the kids after the summer program is that their teachers during the regular school year usually do not maintain the interest in math and science that we create during the summer program. The teachers are too busy trying to control student behavior and too inclined toward lecturing to continue the problem-based education we start in the summer.

It is important to interest Indian students in math and science before they get to college. Every school and every teacher needs to focus on the issues that concern Indian young people and that need to be addressed in Indian communities. Strengthening our cultures, traditions, and languages will aid education, and education can strengthen culture, tradition, and language, as long as we can protect them from outside exploitation. We need to promote more dialogue between our youth and our elders. Linking the knowledge that Indian youth gain from formal education with the wisdom of elders is key to helping communities. Each of us needs to pass on our knowledge to younger people. We need to find ways of linking science and tradition to create new approaches to all of the issues described above.

Let me return to environmental issues as an example of what needs to be done and how it might be accomplished. We consider ourselves the protectors of Mother Earth—"Cuua-Sla-Quem," as we say it in my language. Healthy natural environments require balance and harmony of interconnections and interrelationships. Can we actually protect Mother Earth when even our own lands are being gradually squeezed by developers and companies and individuals who want to exploit single resources and who are willing to break the balances that Mother Earth strives for, all for the sake of the mighty dollar? The destruction of streams, wetlands, and whole ecosystems on reservations due to dumping, mining, overgrazing and livestock waste, and other forms of land and water pollution is ongoing and growing. Improving tribal environmental resource management is vitally important. We also need to improve our ability to deal with biological resources through means such as better livestock control systems and more effective disease prevention and control.

What are some of the problems in promoting an understanding of traditional Indian approaches to these issues and in linking them to modern scientific approaches? The lack of Native Americans trained in relevant disciplines is one major problem. Differences between mainstream science and Indian people in their approach to the environment are fundamental barriers to increasing the numbers of Indians with environmental science skills. Traditional mainstream scientists see no connection between heart and science; Indian tradition says that they are inseparable. Many white scientists also still dismiss traditional Indian strategies for working with the environment; the unconscious persistence of stereotypes of precontact Indians as primitive savages leads to the dismissal of contributions of Native tradition to science.

Some non-Indian scientists, however, have adopted perspectives on life and nature that fit with those of Indian traditions. This is still a minority perspective, but it is a growing one. For example, a few years ago I heard Lorraine Eisley, a distinguished professor from the University of Pennsylvania, speak at the National Association of State Universities and Land-Grant Colleges (NASULGC) conference about water management issues and opportunities. This is one of the things she said: "If there is magic on this planet, it is in water. Water fills our bodies, and it is the solvent of life. It makes the beauty and substance of clouds and dew. It is the strength of thunderstorms and ocean waves. It absorbs the sun's energy and makes our weather. It is life-giving rain and snow and also the fury of hurricanes along our coasts, floods down our water courses, and monsoons across the ocean. It awakens dormant life and brings the miracle of new growth." Dr. Eisley's words could easily have come from someone rooted in traditional Indian culture. Water surely is the stuff of life and the stuff of nations and of commerce, of poetry and of science. Of all things that are essential to us all, water stands first. As mainstream science evolves, it may be moving closer to the Indian perspective on matters such as the sanctity of the waters we all share.

Indian students and educated Indian professionals have some insights into the problems of Indian communities and of the world; Indian elders and grass-roots community members have some other insights. As much as it may pain us to admit it, given past history and current realities, even non-Indian scientists, leaders, and community members may have some unique insights to contribute to Indian people. How to get these groups to understand each other and work together is one big question. How to get universities as institutions and science as a field to collaborate with, rather than dictate to, Indian communities is another. We have a lot of work to do to make these things happen. Succeeding at these issues will require all of us to be open to new ideas and new approaches while maintaining insight into our history and our traditions.

Dean Howard Smith and Joseph S. Anderson

13. Managing Tribal Assets

Developing Long-Term Strategic Plans

As Native American tribes move toward self-determination of their governments and self-sufficiency of their peoples, they face daunting problems: unemployment rates as high as 90%; related social and health issues unseen elsewhere in the United States and Canada; and limited financial assets. To address these problems, tribes clearly need to develop long-term strategic plans. In recent years some tribes have begun earning substantial dollars through gaming operations. Although these funds certainly can assist with community development, these tribes still face the challenge of using all of their assets, financial and otherwise, to build vibrant communities after many years of destitution. So they still need to develop a long-term strategic community development plan.

The development-planning process is really, in the broadest sense, an educational process. Bringing together disparate ideas and views in order to create an agreed-upon whole is the main goal. Accomplishing this requires education of the planning team and of all participants concerning the issues at hand and the possible interconnections between projects.

Traditional economic development tools are useful mainly for communities that already have substantial economic activity. Tribal communities generally lack that. In addition, the extreme social and health issues present in many Indian communities lie beyond the scope of the usual economic analysis methods. To succeed, a development plan for an Indian community needs to include all community development issues—health, education, substance abuse, crime, and others—rather than taking only a narrow economic focus.

All Indian community development projects also need to incorporate both economic and cultural goals and perspectives if they are to have a chance of success. When tribal development plans are conceived externally by members of the dominant culture, they tend to reflect the beliefs, aspirations, and values of their authors rather than those of the tribe. Projects that may seem potentially highly profitable may be unacceptable to Indian community leaders and members for cultural reasons.

Any Indian community development strategy must also take into account at least two levels of government not usually involved in local community development strategies: tribal and federal. Most individual tribe members have little chance of obtaining the capital for business projects without a commitment from the tribal government as either a lender or as a guarantor of a private loan. In addition, whether the intent is to develop private businesses or to develop tribally owned businesses, past, present, and future tribal politics need to be accounted for in any long-term plan. Federal responsibilities due to treaty obligations also need to be considered and incorporated into the plans. Historical and current interference from the federal government in tribal activities, and resulting community distrust, also need to be addressed. On many reservations, various branches of the federal government, led by the BIA in the United States, oversee or control many of the resources available for development. Those agencies have a justifiable reputation among Indian people for short-term thinking, inept management, and failure to take the true interests of Indian communities as their first priority. Strategies for working with those federal agencies and gaining access to the resources they control must be incorporated into the economic development plan.

The National Executive Education Program for Native American Leadership (NEEPNAL) and the Center for American Indian Economic Development (CAIED) have developed a new method for aiding tribes to cultivate community development plans that will work in their unique circumstances. In the NEEPNAL/CAIED approach, a brief background discussion of some of the issues involved in developing Native American economies is provided to the community to aid the tribe in developing a long-term strategic plan. Extensive interviews and workshops are then held for a wide representation of tribal members to reach a consensus on their vision for the next 5, 10, and 20 years. Once an overall vision is expressed, a menu of interwoven economic, social, and cultural projects is developed to achieve it.

Background of Tribal Community Development

Dean Howard Smith created the model that is the basis for the NEEP-NAL/CAIED approach. Mainstream economists argue that progression through a five-stage process is necessary when developing a sustainable local economy. The five stages are these: (1) Exports out of the community are used to cover the cost of things that need to be imported into it. Tourism, agricultural and forest products, gaming, mining revenues and royalties, and federal transfers and treaty obligation payments are common tribal exports. (2) Local production is substituted for some imports. One of the most important examples is the local development of a retail sector. The drain of tribal resources to off-reservation border towns depletes reservation economies, so creating retail services in the local community helps to expand the community economy. The Fort Belknap community in Montana, for instance, substituted fence posts they made themselves using locally harvested timber for ones that they had been buying from off-reservation suppliers. Doing so saved the tribe money and created jobs for tribal members. (3) New and improved products are developed. The import-substitution process may lead to new technologies, entrepreneurial activity, or a reversal of comparative advantages formerly held by external suppliers. (4) New export markets are developed for import-substitute and newly developed products. (5) The cycle begins again as new exports are used to subsidize new imports that improve the standard of living and create new economic opportunities.

Smith has extended the Jacobs model by invoking social theory to show that economic development and cultural integrity can be supportive of each other. This theory views a society as a fabric of intertwining subsystems that include the economic, the familial, the spiritual, the political, the environmental, and the recreational. This theory indicates that when one subsystem is disrupted from the outside the remaining subsystems will also change to achieve a new balance. The U.S. government's reservation policies over the last 100 or so years have drastically altered the economic subsystem of many tribes, and, as the model predicts, this has changed every other aspect of tribal communities. Plains tribes, for instance, who had once met their needs primarily by harvesting buffalo, had to adjust to a new subsistence-level economic subsystem built on federal transfers of dollars, goods, and services. With the loss of an active, independent economy came drastic spontaneous alterations in other social subsystems in Plains communities. Leadership, familial, educational, recreational, and spiritual systems were all disrupted by the loss of the nomadic hunting lifestyle. A downward spiral of all aspects of community health began.

Community development approaches that address all subsystems at once can successfully improve community economics while at the same time maintaining and revitalizing community culture. If, for example, incomes and tribal profits can be increased, part of that increase could be used to finance language programs. Language programs would promote familiarity with traditional cultural values, improve individuals' sense of self-worth, and improve K-12 graduation rates. Higher rates of graduation would yield a better-skilled workforce, making further economic development more likely. An upward spiral of increasing community well-being would be initiated.

An Integrated Approach to Community Development

For simplicity sake, community functioning can be seen as made up of six parts: the economic, the political, the educational, the social, the cultural, and the financial. We will outline these one by one.

The Economic Subsystem

Economic development cannot be generated independently of other community systems. Instead, as will become clear, economic activity is best addressed by way of projects aimed at other community functions. Economic activity is simply a means to the end of creating a healthy, vibrant community. Profitability must therefore be viewed from a broader perspective then simply an accounting one. Scarce resources cannot be devoted to pure job creation. However, sustainable economic activity within a systems perspective cannot be understood with simple profit-and-loss accounting. Consider a new tribal enterprise that will provide employment for a group of community members who currently have no jobs and who are receiving $50,000 in social services from the tribal government. Suppose, further, that the new tribal business will lose $10,000 a year. If the formerly unemployed tribal members earn enough from the enterprise to support themselves, the tribe realizes a $40,000 savings overall, even though the business is not directly profitable. Combine this savings with the positive personal and social consequences of the tribal members' earning their own incomes and it becomes clear that this project would be very worthwhile from the tribe's perspective. As this example shows, the triad of business profits/losses, jobs, and provision of community services could create apparent conflicts for tribes if a pure accounting perspective is used, but it can be integrated effectively if a systems perspective is taken. An overall vision that incorporates the needs of a tribe across all community subsystems has to guide the analysis of all potential projects; only then can tribal leadership and community members make good decisions.

The Political Subsystem

An example of how differences in political systems influence community development plans is that some tribes have a strong separation between economic and political activities and others do not. For instance, some tribes have tribal businesses that are operated by boards of directors made up of tribal members and outsiders, with most board members uninvolved in tribal government. Other tribes have businesses that are ultimately run by the tribal government itself. Where a general separation of economic and political systems exists, development plans can be conceived and executed relatively independently of the dynamics of community politics; where such separation does not exist, the political process must be invoked to help direct the strategic planning process and must be considered while designing and executing projects.

The Educational Subsystem

Obviously, the viability of long-term strategic plans rests on the quality of the skills and expertise available in the community. Educational approaches can also be vitally important to improving social conditions. Therefore, an analysis of the educational system is a requirement for developing effective community development strategies. Quality education for Indian students includes both successful training in standard academic skills and cultural training that maintains the viability of the tribe. There needs to be recognition that language and cultural programs feed positively into the health of other social subsystems in Indian communities, and such programs need to be incorporated into community strategic plans. Higher-education scholarship programs should also be tailored to the future needs of the tribe for skilled workers. Given limited resources, a tribe should set up the scholarship programs to favor particular skills—for example, range management or horticulture—that fit well with economic opportunities and plans.

The Social Subsystem

For the sake of simplicity, we will treat this as a catchall subsystem that includes all social issues and social service programs. Elder care, day care, health care, substance abuse treatment and prevention, spousal and child abuse treatment and prevention, criminal justice, and recreation are examples. Understanding the current social situation of a community and designing programs to address it and improve it in the future are important aspects of any long-term strategic plan. If the programs are to have a chance at success, efforts to address social issues must also, as noted above, be integrated with plans and projects for other areas, such as economic development and education.

For example, the Fort Belknap Indian community developed a substance abuse plan that was also an employment initiative. The tribal council determined that unemployment and substance abuse were the two most pressing problems on the reservation. So they developed an integrated plan of action that involved job training in skills needed for planned tribal businesses as part of a comprehensive substance abuse treatment and prevention program for tribe members.

The Cultural Subsystem

The guiding force for all aspects of the strategic plan is the specific culture of the people. Culture is a way of living developed and transmitted by a group of people to subsequent generations. Since the purpose of any strategic plan is to improve the community and lives of the local population, all aspects of the resultant plan must be suitable for and guided by the cultural subsystem of those people. Therefore, a plan for the Havapai people would have to be different from one for the Ogalala Sioux people, even if they swapped reservations. Ultimately, decisions about how to incorporate culture into strategic plans can be made only by members of each tribe. Nonetheless, Indian communities should follow two general guidelines when incorporating culture into community development planning. First, cultural taboos must be identified and considered in planning. For example, if mining is viewed by a large part of the community as a desecration of Mother Earth, then there is no point in investing time and effort toward planning to exploit mineral resources. Second, in addition to setting the limits within which the strategic plan must be developed, cultural strengths and needs must be inventoried and used in planning. For example, revitalizing traditional feast days and ceremonies can both build community unity and, if cultural norms allow, increase tourism income.

The Financial Subsystem

Progress in any of the subsystems discussed above requires financial resources. The strategic plan needs to focus on developing and effectively managing both general and specific economic opportunities. Some examples of specific economic projects have already been given, and more will be given below. General economic development opportunities might include such things as a microlending program for entrepreneurs. Managing financial resources includes having an effective accounting system that accurately tracks funds due and funds paid, productive long- and short-term investment of capital, and a system for planning for future expenditures and receipts. Many tribes lack accounting and financial planning procedures and systems that properly address even basic financial needs.

The Strategic Planning Process

Interviews

The most important part of the overall planning process is the interviewing, which is essential to developing a clear understanding of the existing circumstances, issues, and goals of a community. It is particularly important that the full range of community views be tapped. Extensive interviews with tribal leaders should occur early in the process. It is also important to interview the elders. Moving to the other end of the demographic spectrum, young people should be interviewed as well. For the most part, the initial focus should be on current conditions—for example, financial conditions and the effectiveness of existing economic projects. As the broad issues begin to become clear, later interviews should focus on specific potential future enterprises or activities. Regardless of who is being interviewed, a rough structure should be followed based on four simple questions. First, what is good about the reservation today? Second, what is wrong with the reservation today? Third, what would you like to see on the reservation in 5, 10, and 20 years? Finally, what would you not like to see in 5, 10, and 20 years? The last question is very important from a cultural perspective, because the answers may point toward otherwise hidden cultural taboos or community norms that must be considered in planning.

Secondary Research

Another phase of the process is the examination of relevant documents. Some types of needed information may be easy to come by, such as descriptions of natural resources on a reservation. Other information, such as reliable figures on unemployment rates, may be more difficult to obtain. In any case, the more hard, reliable data one can obtain the better the resultant understanding of both existing community circumstances and potential levers for future community development.

Planning Workshops

Following an initial round of interviews and the gathering of secondary information, a workshop should be held with appropriate tribal representatives. Not all attendees need to have been interviewed previously. When NEEPNAL and CAIED are involved in community planning, the staff present an initial outline for a strategic plan in this workshop. We outline the five-stage Jacobs model and—based on the understanding of the resources, conditions, needs, and aspirations of the tribe we have developed through the information-gathering phase of the planning process—the staff drafts a potential general plan of action for the community. Example projects from other communities are described to allow the audience to focus on the process of economic development.

Once the formal presentation is completed, the staff facilitates an open discussion based on the same four basic questions used in the interviews. One NEEPNAL/CAIED staff member facilitates the strategic planning discussion, and a second records the thoughts and ideas the community members offer. This session may be the very first time that heads of particular tribal bureaus and other community members have discussed strategic issues together. We often suggest that a regularly scheduled, formal strategic planning session based on the workshop model be added to the system of tribal governance.

A concise vision statement that touches on every subsystem discussed above is created in collaboration with the tribe. It should include specific targets in each priority area. For example, it might state that high school dropout and unemployment rates will be reduced by more than half from the current rates. The targets in the vision statement set the stage for development of a detailed strategic plan.

Creating the Menu of Projects

Ideas for all of the following items should have been discussed during the planning workshop: tribal enterprises, private enterprises, community projects, education projects, health care issues, and governance modifications. Some projects may be mutually exclusive for financial or other reasons, and others will seem obviously complementary. Linkages and conflicts should be explicated. Based on the vision statement and its targets, and the linkages and conflicts identified among projects from the workshop, certain projects should tentatively be selected for action. A description of those projects, their goals, requirements, and interconnections is written and forwarded to tribal representatives for further refinement. The tribal government then determines which projects to pursue. At this point, detailed business plans are developed for the economic activities to determine the feasibility of various projects. Similarly, plans and budgets are prepared for the related nonbusiness activities. Then the process moves to the action phase, where the selected projects are actually implemented and evaluated.

The process described in this chapter has been successfully completed by various NEEPNAL/CAIED partner tribes. The end result of a strategic plan is actually only the initial step on the path toward self-sufficiency and self-determination. It is, though, a vital step. In order to take this step, the tribal community must look forward and be ready to take the risks necessary to reach into the future. Creating the vision of what that future should hold is perhaps the most important step. The economic, community, cultural, and other projects within the body of the strategic plan are simply means toward the end of reaching the vision of the people.

Gerri Shangreaux

14. On the Front Lines of Indian Health

Practical and Political Issues in Providing
Community Health Care

I would first like to tell you about my own journey to becoming a faculty member in medical education to illustrate the difficulties many Native people encounter in trying to succeed in education and in the professional world. I will use my personal story to lead into a discussion of the problems that occur in efforts to improve Indian health.

I grew up on the Pine Ridge Reservation in South Dakota, where I spent 12 years attending the mission school in Marty, South Dakota. Unlike many of the authors in this book, who were probably honor students, I am one of those people who initially struggled a great deal in school. In that respect, I think I represent a lot of Indian people who can make it in formal education, but only after years of struggle. I think some of us have to heal and come to terms with what has been stripped from us before we can be ready to succeed in school. We are the product of many decades of failed federal Indian policies— relocations, mission schools, boarding schools, imposed values, and enforced external control. It certainly took years for me to understand who I am and what contributions I can make to Lakota and other Indian peoples.

When I was in high school, I told my high school counselor, Sister Williams, that I wanted to go to college and become a nurse or a social worker. She responded, "You are just average. You will never be able to go to college." She had a huge poster in her office, a board that had every student's name on it. Next to each name it said "Best," or "Worst," or "Average." Next to my name was "Average," and that led her to say that I would never be able to go to college. I was very distressed by what she said. I might have believed her and given up, but just then my father put my picture into the local newspaper with a caption that said I was going to become a nurse. I did not know what to do. I had to find a way to become a nurse or I felt that I could not live at Pine Ridge again. Eventually I found a Bureau of Indian Affairs relocation program that sent me to Los Angeles to become a nurse's aide.

In Los Angeles, a black nurse I worked with told me that she, too, had been told that she could never go to college. So, like me, she also started as a nurse's aide. By going to community college during her off-hours, though, she eventually became a licensed practical nurse (LPN). That was the first time I had ever heard of community colleges. I followed the suggestion of the nurse who befriended me and started attending community college classes after work. It was a struggle, but I finally did become an LPN at age 24. Having become a nurse, I finally felt I could return to the Pine Ridge Reservation and face my family and friends.

I worked as an LPN for a couple of years at Pine Ridge before deciding that I needed to obtain more education if I was going to accomplish the kinds of things I really wanted to do. I was interested in going to medical school but did not have a strong enough academic background to get admitted. Then someone, I still do not know who, sent my name to a physician's assistant (PA) training program for Native Americans at the University of New Mexico. Many people are unfamiliar with the profession of physician's assistant. It is a position in the health care field that is pretty much midway between the traditional role of the physician and the traditional role of the nurse. Like medical doctors (MDs), physician's assistants are supervised by MDs, provide support to MDs, and follow up on decisions and treatment plans of MDs. I got the application for the University of New Mexico program on the day of the deadline and had to scramble to organize the materials and send them out. I got it done, though, and was among 10 out of 200 applicants accepted into the program.

There were eight different tribes represented in my class, and that was when I began to learn a bit about different tribes' cultures, histories, and health care needs. Because the program was in New Mexico, I became especially involved with the Navajo tribe. I would travel 90 miles back and forth between Albuquerque and the Navajo reservation in a dilapidated car. It was very enlightening because the Navajo belief system is very different from the Lakota one. The contrast between our tribes really helped me understand who I am as a Lakota woman. I feel very honored to have had the experience of being partially trained on the Navajo reservation.

After graduating from the physician's assistant program, I initially worked with urban Indians in direct health care. The urban Indian setting was also a cultural learning experience because it meant working with multiple Indian groups and with some unique health issues that occur mainly in urban settings. I had to learn how to deal effectively with many different Indian cultures. Just because I am Lakota does not mean I understand everything about every other Indian tribe. This is something that non-Indians often do not understand: The various tribes differ so much in their histories, cultures, current conditions, available resources, community dynamics, and other things that there is no such thing as *the* Native American experience. I had to learn over time what I understood and was comfortable with and how to network with other people who have expertise with the tribes and with issues that I am less knowledgeable about.

I worked in the urban Indian health program for about 8 years, developing and applying health programs for Native Americans at the grass-roots level. It is very disturbing to see the statistics on the health of Native people; we are near the bottom on many indices of health. American Indians have the shortest average life span, the highest accident and injury rates, and the highest levels of diabetes of any U.S. ethnic group. Native Americans suffer from blindness and infant mortality at rates significantly higher than the U.S. national average. I dealt with all of these problems and more while working in health programs on Pine Ridge, on the Navajo reservation, and for urban Indians.

It troubled me to see the high levels of illness and death among Native people in the clinics and homes where I worked. I came to realize that better efforts at prevention of health problems among Native people are needed. I saw that lack of knowledge was a major reason why a lot of the health problems existed among the Indian people with whom I worked. I came to believe that one of the best things I could possibly do would be to help educate people in Indian communities about health maintenance and health promotion. We all know that preventing is better than curing, but the way that the health care system is financed and the way that the medical establishment is set up emphasize treatment of existing problems much more than efforts to keep problems from occurring. Because of my interest in prevention, I began to develop a community health education curriculum.

One example of the education work I started doing is a curriculum for a course called "Nutrition for Native Americans." Nutrition education is near the bottom of the list of priorities in the field of medicine. Yet, nutrition is very important to health and is especially an issue for Native people. Most American Indians have abandoned traditional foods only to find that many modern foods are worse for them than for non-Native people. Obesity, for instance, is an important factor for the likelihood of developing diabetes and hypertension. Some Native groups seem to process calories much more efficiently than non-Native people. When Indians switched from their traditional diets to calorie- and fat-rich mainstream diets, their bodies did not stop being efficient at using that food, and levels of obesity and the illnesses it can trigger increased tremendously. There are other nutrition-related health problems among Native people besides the example I just gave, but because very few Native Americans work in the fields of nutrition education and nutrition research, little work has been done to investigate these problems. In my opinion, these are two of the most important health fields that could do the most good for Native people. We need to do more to increase the numbers of Native people pursuing them.

I presented my "Nutrition for Native Americans" curriculum to the Indian communities, and there was opposition at first. My nutrition training got caught up in tribal politics and factions. But as Frank Dukepoo said in Chapter 6, to accomplish anything in Indian education or Indian community development, you have got to stick your neck out and risk getting your head chopped off. I have had my head chopped off many times while trying to push for changes in Indian community health programs and Indian health education. I persisted with my nutrition curriculum despite the initial resistance and criticism and was finally able to win the general support of the communities with which I was working. Through the education programs, some community members changed their eating habits and managed to avoid health problems or became healthier if they already had nutrition-related problems. The success of my health education courses led one of the tribal colleges to approach me and say, "We would like you to teach at our college."

I thought at first that the college wanted me just to do a one-shot workshop, but they actually wanted me to be a professor. I agreed to try, and that is how I ended up being a faculty member. Before I knew it, I was promoted to dean of the college. I did not even really know what it involved when I took the position, but I did a lot of research, learned on the job, and found some ways to improve the effectiveness of the college as a whole.

One problem I have encountered again and again both at that tribal college and now at the University of South Dakota is that institutions of higher education often think they understand the problems of Indian communities. They are often wrong. The administration and faculty typically have not been out on the front lines working directly with Indian health projects or other Indian community needs, and they generally do not have strong ties to any

Indian community. Yet, they still often believe that they understand what the problems are, what causes them, and what needs to be done to effectively address them.

Even the tribal community college I worked for often did not understand the health needs of its own community or how to develop and present health programs so that they would be accepted and used. This became so frustrating that I finally felt I had to leave that school. I moved on to the University of South Dakota.

I see my role as a bridge for the gap between Indian communities and the medical education establishment. I have been on the front lines of Indian health for most of my adult life, which has given me a different perspective than that of most people in medical education. When you work every day with Indian patients, attend various types of functions and activities in Indian communities, and listen to the views of different Indian community groups every week, you learn a great deal that you cannot get out of books. When people in an Indian community raise an issue, you know what they are talking about and why, and you understand the context of all of the other things that relate to that particular issue. So you are better placed to translate the health goals and needs of Indian communities into workable curricula, projects, or programs.

The following example illustrates how my approach to education differs from that of most people in the physician's assistant program: There is a renal dialysis unit at Pine Ridge, and I take students there to learn about renal disease among Native people and how to treat it. This is part of a new concept, new at least to the PA program, that I have introduced called problem-based learning. It includes a lot of hands-on learning and cooperative education. I push for this method because it fits with the traditional Lakota approach of sharing. These days, however, even our own people do not cooperate much of the time. Often, in these modern times, we do not practice what our own traditional systems of values teach us. As a Native American who has been out on the front lines of Indian health care for years, I understand the importance of cooperation among health providers as well as among health providers, patients, and families. With renal patients or patients with other illnesses, maintaining or improving the patients' health means dealing with their families and their communities as well. For instance, how do you change a patient's diet unless the family changes the types of food they buy and prepare? So understanding how to share medical knowledge and how to both teach and learn from all kinds of people are very important.

My problem-based, cooperative learning approach to renal disease was difficult for many of my students at first. Toward the end of the semester, though, they began to get better at it and even began to like it. Moreover, most of those students had near-perfect final examination scores and consequently received A's for course grades. In the end, their success attests that, as a teacher, I was able to succeed in teaching them both specific course content and an approach to gathering, interpreting, and using information that will generally help make them better health care providers.

Other authors in this book have talked about the important issue of the hoops and politics of the alien system of higher education that make life difficult for Indian faculty members. Those things are what I am trying to work through right now as a novice assistant professor. Many times I have thought about quitting, about just giving up. Sometimes, when I get really frustrated, I think the university is hindering me rather than helping me to accomplish things. My specific agenda is to try to work on improving health in Indian communities. The university claims that this is also one of their goals, but fundraising, external political powers, internal turf battles, and bureaucratic inertia all interfere with pursuing that goal. For example, I want to incorporate some Indian community and cultural content into the University of South Dakota Physician Assistant's Training Program, in which I now teach. When I was hired, I was promised that I would be able to do such a thing. But it has been hard to actually get the institution to make any concrete changes or additions to the program.

Cultural difference is part of the problem for me. I am just beginning to learn how things are actually done at my institution and how the culture of the faculty and the administration operates. If there was a visible line with assimilation on one side and tradition on the other, somewhere from the middle of that continuum on over toward the side of tradition is where I would stand. I also realize, though, that the more time I spend in a non-Native university system the more I am pulled toward assimilation. The struggle to remain Lakota while working in a mainstream system is a constant battle for me and is probably an issue for most Native educators.

Eventually, I want to go home to Pine Ridge. I constantly have visions, and one is to create strong basic science programs on my home reservation. Many of the state colleges and universities in South Dakota and North Dakota and other northern plains areas have a difficult time recruiting and retaining Indian students. Part of the reason is that many Indian students lack the basic science education in high school to be able to succeed in college science courses or health profession degree programs. My goal is to someday go back and teach some of the basic science courses at a tribal college. There are too few Native American instructors at tribal colleges, especially in the sciences, and this is one of the things I would like to help change in a few years.

The other related area with which I have become more involved is health research for Native people. At one time, even just a century ago, the Lakota people were extremely healthy, but now we have tremendous health problems, especially with diabetes, hypertension, and kidney disease. Diabetes and hypertension go hand in hand, are more common among Indians than among other groups, and tend to result in kidney disease. I am working with a small grant now to research these three diseases among Indians. I want to find out why such high rates of these illnesses occur among Indians and, more importantly, how to prevent them.

Many of our tribes have been researched to death but to little good effect. We have to gather the right information and then put it to effective use. Non-Indian faculty members and program directors have generally not done that, so it is up to Indian people to do it for themselves. So my goal for the immediate future is to do some very useful health research and put the knowledge I gain into action back on the front lines.

Ron Jamieson

15. Innovative Strategies for Promoting Development in Indian Communities

I want to tell you just a little about myself and a little of the history of how I became involved with the Bank of Montreal. First of all, I am a Mohawk. I was born and raised at the Six Nations Reserve in Ontario, Canada. I still live at Six Nations. I have never lived anywhere but Six Nations. Six Nations, for those who are not familiar with it, is the largest reserve by population in Canada. We have 18,000 members in our nation, 12,000 of whom reside on our territory. Many of us joke that we hope the other 6,000 do not come home because we do not have enough houses for them.

You may wonder what a banker has to do with integrating Indian community needs with education. I will try to answer that question in this chapter. When I arrived at the conference from which this book evolved, I ran into Keith, who said, "Gee, Ron, I hardly recognized you without your suit." I usually do wear a suit every day. In fact, back at Six Nations, where I live on the reserve, they call me Mohawk in a Suit. It is part of the uniform of banking and, of course, one of the obstacles that I have had to overcome to deal successfully with Native people. But we need Natives in suits, even Natives in banks, if we are going to succeed in advancing Indian community well-being.

I was originally a chemist, then I became a stockbroker, and now I am a banker. I am not going to take you through all of the horror stories, but I will tell you that there has never been any love lost between Native Canadians and the banks. After all, banks have never done anything for Native people. That was certainly my view before I became personally involved in the banking industry. Seven years ago, the vice-chairman of the Bank of Montreal called me and said, "Ron, I would like to talk to you and tell you what we are planning to do in Aboriginal banking." At the time, I was running a brokerage firm in downtown Toronto. I told him, very frankly, that I was not interested in whatever he was planning to do because I felt that, whatever it was, it would be window dressing and would not really accomplish much. I was not going to be the guy sitting in an office somewhere posing as the symbolic "resident Indian" in their huge institution.

The Bank of Montreal today has 33,000 employees, operates in 80 countries, and has assets of about 200 billion dollars. So it is a very large organization, and I was very, very suspicious of anything that they were planning on launching that dealt with banking for Native Canadians. I told the vice-chairman to "forget it," that I was not interested. Besides, I really was not looking to change jobs since I was doing very well at the time as a stockbroker. The vice-chairman persevered, however; about two weeks after our first telephone conversation, he called back and said, "Ron, let's at least have breakfast, and maybe you can provide me with some advice." So I said to myself, "Well, it *is* a free breakfast from a banker, and you rarely get anything free from one of them." So I decided to go and have breakfast with him, but I remained very suspicious.

I went to the 68th floor of the bank tower in downtown Toronto and met with the vice-chairman at probably one of the nicest dining rooms I have ever been in. We ended up spending about two hours together. At the end of our discussion, I at least believed that he as an individual was sincere, but I also knew by then that he had no knowledge of the Indian Act or of the huge problems and tensions surrounding the relationship between Aboriginal and non-Aboriginal people in Canada. I thought that he really did not know what he was getting into and that, as soon as he found out, he was going to run for cover. It was one thing to have one executive interested in doing new things in Aboriginal banking, but it was another to actually get those things operating. There are a lot of other people involved between the vice-chairman and the grass-roots operations of the 1,200 branches of the Bank of Montreal in Canada. Yet, I kept meeting with him, questioning him in detail and trying to educate him about the nature of the issues. We had a series of discussions over a couple of months. By the end of that time, I was somewhat intrigued. I still thought that his plans for Aboriginal banking were going to be a major bust, but I did finally agree to a 7-month consulting contract on the off-chance that the project might actually succeed.

By the end of my initial 7 months of consulting with the bank, I had discovered that there were many people there who were sincere about wanting to provide banking services to, and develop relationships with, Aboriginal communities. They still did not really understand what they were getting themselves into, but they were at least sincere about wanting to provide better service to Aboriginal communities. If you have to have a starting point for any project, let it be that: Make sure the people involved are at least truly committed to the basic goal. At the end of my first 7 months with the bank, I was asked to join it as a full-time employee. I was interested in the proposal, but before deciding, I discussed the bank's ideas and its offer to me with the elders and clan mothers at Six Nations. They thought that I could make a difference, that I could make changes in the attitudes of, and the relationships between, Aboriginal people and the banks in Canada. So I ended up accepting the bank's offer to join its leadership full-time as the Vice President for Aboriginal Banking.

I should explain, for those from the United States who may not be very familiar with the term, that we often use the word "Aboriginal" as the label for Native people in Canada because of the number of different Native groups that exist there. At my bank, for instance, we work with the people of the high Arctic; with the Innu people of northern Quebec and northern Labrador; with the Inuit people from the eastern Arctic; with the Inewvialowit people from the western Arctic; and, of course, with all of the various First Nations people across the lower and middle tiers of Canada. The diversity of clients creates a tremendous variety of challenges. The Aboriginal communities in the high north of Canada are, for instance, very remote; flying is the only way to get to many of them. As a consequence, no matter what business you are in, service delivery to some of those northern communities becomes very, very difficult.

So how was one Mohawk from southern Ontario going to satisfy, or at least attempt to satisfy, the banking needs of such a very diverse group of people who were stretched over a very huge area across the country and who had very different goals and issues? The first thing we did was to put together what we called the Circle of Aboriginal Business Leaders. These are men and women of all types of Aboriginal descent who gather on a quarterly basis to provide us with advice on the programs that we are executing or planning. With that group we have planned not only programs for the delivery of financial services but also training programs for preparing Aboriginal people for jobs in banking and for moving some of them into positions of authority in the bank.

When I joined the Bank of Montreal 5 years ago, we had 110 employees of Aboriginal descent out of 30,000 total employees—a dismal record, in my view. Today, we have 560 Aboriginals working for the bank, and over 30% of them are in management or executive positions. In addition, we have sponsored many training programs across Canada to attract Aboriginal people to the fields of finance and accounting and to other disciplines that are going to be desperately needed for the development of our communities. If you really want to make a change in an institution as large as the Bank of Montreal, the most effective way to do so is to get a lot of like-minded people on the inside. You have to both understand what is important to the existing decision makers and bring in as many of your own people (or at least people who share your people's views) as possible. If you can do those two things, you can change an institution from the inside much more quickly and thoroughly than you could from the outside.

Having put together the Circle of Aboriginal Business Leaders, we then hired Managers of Aboriginal Banking for each of the Bank of Montreal's divisions across Canada. Then we began our outreach to Aboriginal communities. Five years ago, we had one branch in all of Canada that was serving an Aboriginal community. Today, we have 16 in various parts of the country. The important thing about these branches is that they provide welcoming environments to Native people. In every one of those branches, we have at least one person who speaks the community's traditional language. This is done both to increase people's comfort with us and to improve the quality of our service to them.

But even with that kind of progress, we were still faced with difficult, some would say insurmountable, problems in providing loans to Aboriginal individuals and groups. Those problems come from the provisions of the Indian Act. I do not have a detailed understanding of the laws that pertain to lending on Indian reservations in the United States, but I do know that the legal obstacles are generally similar to the ones in Canada. The main issue is that Native individuals and governments are prohibited by law from using their reserve lands as collateral for a loan, and many do not have anything else they can use. Banks do not like to make unsecured loans (that is, loans where the person or group receiving the loan does not put up something of value that the bank can take if the loan is not repaid on time), except to people who already have a lot of money. So Native individuals, Native corporations, and band governments and tribal councils generally cannot get bank loans.

Previously, government guarantees were the only thing that would convince banks to provide loans to most Natives. In my 5 years with the bank, we have developed business loan programs and housing loan programs in seven Aboriginal communities in Canada without any government involvement whatsoever. That has never been done before, at least not in Canada. Instead, we use something we call central mortgage and housing guarantees in place of ministerial (government) guarantees or direct collateral. We have set up, and continue to set up, relationships directly between the bank and the governments of Aboriginal communities—typically a band council or an Inuit community council. This is the way the loans work: Since banks cannot take title to reserve land, Aboriginal individuals or groups who want a loan give the Aboriginal community government the right to take their land if the loan is not repaid as promised. The government then pledges to the bank that they will take that land and sell it to another band or community member to raise money to cover the defaulted loan. The truth is that we would have a hard time enforcing an Aboriginal government's promise if they ended up not voluntarily honoring it, so the program really does depend on trust.

We have also launched a related program to finance educational facilities in Aboriginal communities. Previously in Canada you had to go on a capital allocation waiting list at the Department of Indian Affairs (DIA) to get money to construct schools in Aboriginal communities. I can tell you that right now the list has over 50 requests for schools on it; the average price to build each of those schools would be 6 million dollars. So it would require approximately 300 million dollars to meet Aboriginal communities' current requests for educational facilities. The DIA allocates only 110 million dollars each year toward satisfying those building needs. Since that is less than what would be required just to meet the existing need for schools, and since requests for additional schools keep growing each year, the DIA and Aboriginal communities will never be able to catch up. Observing that need and having heard from our Circle of Aboriginal Business Leaders advisory group and others that promoting education is crucial to the development of Aboriginal communities in all respects, we decided to try to devise a way to finance reserve schools. We succeeded in our efforts, again without federal or provincial government involvement. The Bank of Montreal has begun loaning money for immediate school construction in Aboriginal communities that will be repaid with the dollars that the communities will save in the future on the tuition costs they are now paying for their children to attend schools in off-reserve school districts. We and the participating First Nations governments jointly use our funding to build needed schools on the reserves. When the schools are located on the reserve, the staff can be Native, the curriculum can be developed by the community, and the needs of both the community and our young Native population can be better met. Creative solutions like this one that give control to Aboriginal communities are, to me, the way to ensure that the future prospects of those communities are better than their recent histories.

The Bank of Montreal is also expanding its activities to the United States and Mexico. We own a bank in the United States called Harris Bank, which is located primarily in the Chicago area but also operates in Arizona and Florida. A few years ago, we also bought a portion of the largest bank in Mexico. We have already visited some Native leaders in the United States and Mexico to see what kind of outreach we might be able to do with their communities.

I am not going to tell you that doing any of the things I described above was easy. It was not. In addition to the practical and technical issues we had to deal with, we also had to engage in a lot of persuasion; there were a lot of skeptics both in the bank and in the Aboriginal communities. But I can also tell you that with the loan portfolio I am responsible for today, which runs into the hundreds of millions of dollars, the loan losses in that portfolio are less than half, less than 50%, of the loan losses the bank experiences overall. That is the kind of evidence that has convinced the hardheaded financial types in the bank to keep these kinds of programs going. I can promise you that we *will* keep them going. We intend to hire more Aboriginal people. We intend to move those people into more senior levels of management. We intend to make more loans for a broader range of purposes to Aboriginal individuals and groups. We are going to create more partnerships with Aboriginal communities. And we are going to create more programs to build on the limited progress we have made up to this point in getting needed financial services and financial training to Native people. The challenges in attempting to find creative ways to fulfill the needs of Aboriginal communities are great but so, too, are the rewards.

Part 4

The Land, the People, and Science

Keith James

16. Sons of the Sun, Daughters of the Earth

Indian groups in North America extended, and still extend, from very warm climes—both jungles and deserts—to places deep in the northern frigid zones. Some authors in this volume come from extreme climatic zones— Ofelia Zepeda out of the Sonoran desert and Lillian Dyck from chilly Saskatchewan—while others come from the more temperate areas in between. Indian people have always lived in the mountains, on the plains, near the ocean, in the woodlands. The tribes residing in these different environments had lifestyles and cultures that were adapted to their particular place. But they also created their places through their cultures; for example, the horse was modified into the Indian pony by the Plains tribes and the desert was cultivated by the tribes dwelling there.

In Chapter 1, I noted some major environmental problems in Indian communities. Other contributors have made reference to additional problems or have described environmental resource management needs and opportunities that are going unmet in Indian communities. I could give many other examples of pollution and environmental degradation, and in each case mainstream scientists or engineers along with mainstream technologies and application of them would be found to have played some substantial role in creating the problem. Few of the scientists and engineers who helped generate the environmental problems in Indian communities have volunteered to help solve them. Perhaps they would help if there were money to be made or if the problem affected mainstream society rather than a relatively small minority group.

As I argued in Chapter 7, scientific techniques and tools may be objective in and of themselves, but the *application* of those techniques and tools is always value laden. Native people, history has shown, cannot rely on promises of scientific objectivity to protect their land any more than they can rely on them to protect their other blessings. Thus, the authors in this section argue that Native communities need their own environmental advisors and experts if they are to mitigate past damage, minimize future harm, and enhance their viability and vigor. Freda Porter-Locklear provides especially compelling examples of pollution problems in Indian communities that are going unaddressed. She, as well as Jhon Goes in Center and Jane Mt. Pleasant, also offers very specific ideas about the types of environmental skills and knowledge that are especially needed, as well as some strategies for increasing the numbers of Indian people skilled in those areas. Each of the succeeding three chapters also argues that general benefits would result if more Indians acquired such skills and knowledge. Porter-Locklear stresses most the interconnectedness of the land, water, and air of Indian and non-Indian communities, which brings with it a need for joint intervention, management, and prevention. Jane Mt. Pleasant makes a strong case for the unique perspectives that Indians could bring to environmental science and practice, perspectives that might generally add to and alter the approaches of the fields in that area.

I am very interested in environmental issues even though my disciplinary training is not in environmental science. Because of that interest, I am aware that some currents within mainstream environmental science already seem to be trending somewhat toward Indian perspectives. The extent to which those currents are becoming, or will become, deep and wide rather than shallow and narrow is very much in question, however. An emphasis on actually bringing Indian people into environmental science professions, rather than using only some elements of their traditional perspectives or knowledge, should help strengthen relevant currents of reform.

As the authors in this section make clear, approaches of Indian cultures to the environment differ from the depictions of those approaches being promoted by some New Age movements and mainstream environmentalists. Traditional Indian environmental views are complex rather than simple, active rather than passively worshipful. These authors argue, though, that one fairly consistent and general difference in the environmental perspectives of traditional indigenous cultures and mainstream science is that many of the precontact changes to the environment by Indian people were informed by a deeper understanding of and a greater respect for the world. Another related difference is, as I mentioned earlier, Native people's more holistic view of the environment and their actions in and on it. Native cultures were and are systems for integrating the human, the social, the natural, and the spiritual. Mainstream society and mainstream science, at least since the Renaissance, have found some benefits from attempting to wall these areas off from each other, such that beliefs in reductionism, specialization, and the possibility of "rational" environmental control have become enshrined in Western world-views. These approaches *have* produced some benefits but at costs that we are beginning to realize may not be tolerable in the long run. Moreover, recent changes in the scope and power of the technologies at the disposal of humans seem to make the existing Western scientific orientation toward partition and short-term outcomes highly risky.

Some people would say that traditional Indian approaches to the environment reflect nothing more than a difference in technology. That is, Indian people did not have the technology to broadly impact or control the environment, so they adopted values focused on accommodation. There may be some truth to that idea, but it is exaggerated, being based on distorted views of how tribes lived before contact with Europeans. Mt. Pleasant's and Goes in Center's chapters are especially useful for countering some of the false perceptions current in mainstream society about Indians' indigenous technologies and Indian societies' sophistication in understanding and modifying their environments. The selection and use of technologies flow from norms and values of cultures at least as much as they shape those norms and values. So if Indian people's technologies were ones that did less harm to life and to the earth, it was partly because they empathized more with all parts of this world; did not conceive of themselves as above, or possessed of a right of dominion over, other life forms; did believe in an obligation of reciprocity with all other entities; and consequently placed great value on care for all aspects of the world. Jane Mt. Pleasant's discussion of the Three Sisters approach to Iroquois agriculture provides a compelling illustration of one traditional Native perspective on the environment. Jhon Goes in Center and Freda Porter-Locklear emphasize Indian environmental empathy in other ways.

Notice, however, that not one of these authors has a global antiscience and antitechnology bias. It is quite the opposite, in fact, since all of them recognize benefits to Indian individuals and communities of particular scientific fields or technological innovations. All have visions, however, of a distinctly Indian version of those fields or of how those technologies could be applied to promise better results for both Indian and non-Indian people.

Despite claims by some that modern science and technologies are either alien to or independent of other major earthly systems, these authors (and many other Indian people) view humans and their works, including science and technology, as components of natural systems (see also Atleo's perspective in Chapter 23). This means that people are as capable of rightness and balance and beauty as any other natural product but that they are also subject to the same biases, limitations, checks, balances, and possible extinctions as other parts. Nature and human nature allow many potential options for our individual and collective ways of connecting to the world. Our task is to find healthy and honorable ones rather than settling for the ones that are most expedient.

Freda Porter-Locklear

17. Water and Water Quality Issues in and for American Indian Communities

I still think back frequently to my 18 years on my parents' farm and the lessons I learned from them. One of the most valuable things I learned was that, when you invest in a hard day's work, you are going to get a marvelous return. My father would say to my siblings and me, "You know it doesn't come easy. Life's hard work." Investing yourself in growing things and feeding people is one of the most valuable ways of living. It is a hard life, though, and small farmers are often poor. I felt there must be more to life than the long hours and meager income of farming. So I decided to become something other than a farmer.

I went to elementary and high schools that had only Indian students. Most of the people who attended those schools did not go on to college, so I really did not have any educational role models. People ask me how, coming from that background, I managed to get a Ph.D. in mathematics. I believe it goes back to the ethic of working hard that my parents taught me, along with the attention I got in the early school grades from some Indian teachers. Without those two things, I certainly would not have been able to be successful academically.

But successful I was. I was the class valedictorian in high school, and that got me an academic scholarship to attend Pembroke State University. After graduating from Pembroke State, I was fortunate enough to receive one of the first graduate fellowships given by the National Science Foundation. That fellowship allowed me to continue on to North Carolina State University, where I received a master's degree in applied mathematics. At first I was not interested in staying in school to pursue a Ph.D. So I went to work as a computer programmer for a few years and then taught for a couple of years.

Finally, though, in 1986, I returned to school at Duke University to work on a Ph.D. in applied mathematics.

When my path to the Ph.D. is described on paper, it sounds much easier than it was. It was, in fact, an uphill battle. As one of the few women, and the only Indian woman, in my Ph.D. program, I had to get used to being unique. Since there is only a handful of other Indian women with Ph.D.'s in mathematics, I have remained unusual. Also, during all of my postsecondary education, I was the mother of two children. As is true for a lot of Indian women, the struggle to balance children with my desire to pursue an education was not easy. It took a lot of determination and a lot of support to make it through.

I remember thinking during my doctoral graduation ceremony, "Is this really true?" I kept pinching myself. To get that Ph.D. after all of the struggle and work was a crowning moment in my life. My whole family was there, and it was an unbelievable day for us all. Based on my experience, I know that Indian students working on degrees in mathematics or the sciences will often feel strange and uncomfortable at first and will have to struggle with conflicting demands to make it through. But my experience shows that you can get used to being one of a kind in the unfamiliar culture of a university mathematics or science department. And the struggle is worth it, both because you will benefit personally from the opportunities the education will give you and because Indian communities desperately need people with mathematical and scientific skills.

Since getting my Ph.D., I have been devoting my time to two types of work. The first is my research work with the Environmental Protection Agency (EPA) in ground water modeling. The second type involves various American Indian Science and Engineering Society (AISES) projects. I cannot say enough good things about AISES and the work that organization does to help Indian students receive an education in science and engineering. I will continue to give my time to help with its projects in any way I can.

I have been told many times that to be a successful doctorate-level professional, you have to devote yourself to your own research first and always. For Indians, that is really hard to do. It is not the way we are reared. As a child, I was taught that sharing with others and caring for friends and family was most important. Having a high level of education does not allow you to simply put those values aside. I remember my own struggles and the people who helped me, and that helps keep me focused on the needs of Indian students and Indian communities. Sometimes, students' demands on my time seem just overwhelming. But I feel it is my responsibility to give back as much as I can to repay the help I received, so I keep trying.

As an Indian Ph.D., I have experienced all of the problems that other authors talk about in their chapters: the denigration of Indian-focused projects; the lip service support from other faculty and from university administrators that is often not backed by concrete action or resources; the shallow understanding of the true conditions in Indian communities or for Indian students; and the pressure to produce the kind of standard scientific products that other faculty have generated and can easily understand. Those things have not been easy to deal with, but I think that if you are an Indian and a scientist you simply have to accept the burden of both doing good scientific work and finding a way to make that work serve Native communities.

Consideration of those two demands leads me, finally, to the topic of water in Indian communities. Why, with training in applied mathematics, did I get into issues of water quality? For several reasons: First, my Lumbee community has a water-based way of life. Because of that, I grew up around water all my life and have always had a love of water. We consider water our most precious environmental resource. My people, though, have experienced many problems with water pollution in recent decades. Awareness of those problems made me interested in working on controlling water pollution. So when the possibility of my doing water quality modeling with the EPA was first raised in 1991, it clicked with me, and I knew that this was an area in which I could happily work for a long time.

Now, this chapter is entitled "Water and Water Quality Issues in and for American Indian Communities," but the truth is that we cannot limit our concerns to inside the boundaries of Indian communities because pollution from surrounding areas breaches those boundaries. With water, as with other parts of nature, everything is connected, and the harm that is done in one place will eventually affect us all. For example, a hurricane that hit North Carolina in 1997 caused electrical outages, and because of loss of power, the city of Fayetteville emptied its wastewater from the treatment plant into the Cape Fear River. That sewage dump affected communities and natural areas along the whole length of the river. The Cape Fear River feeds into the Intercoastal Waterway, which drains into the Atlantic Ocean at Southport. Southport is where many of the Lumbee people have traditionally fished. The fishing season in the previous 2 years had been bad because of other types of pollution. But the raw sewage that the city of Fayetteville dumped in the water made things worse; it literally destroyed the Lumbee fishing area.

The large sewage dump from Fayetteville I just described was unusual, but smaller-scale municipal wastewater overflows are common. They can kill the fish, and they introduce bacteria into the water, such as E. coli, that can make humans very sick.

Another example of how water pollution does not respect community boundaries involves the Lumber River. This is a body of water where the Lumbee people have long fished, that they used to travel from place to place by canoe, and where they swam. Now you rarely see people canoeing, swimming, or fishing in it. A lot of the fish have been killed, and most people would not eat the few remaining fish because of the chemicals they contain. The pollution problems in the Lumber largely stem from farm water runoff. The lands of the Lumbee people are in a farming region in Robertson County, North Carolina. Many pesticides and other agricultural chemicals are used on the mainstream farms that surround the Lumbee lands. Those commercial agricultural chemicals run off of the farm lands and into every body of water in the area. If the farmers used organic fertilizers and natural pest controls, we would not have nearly as much of a water pollution problem.

Hog farm waste is another big issue in my area and has been linked to a number of illnesses. For instance, people who have come into contact with wastewater from hog farms have developed skin lesions and gastrointestinal illnesses. A moratorium on new large-scale livestock operations was recently enacted because health problems from them had become so common. The runoff from agricultural chemicals and animal waste produces high levels of mercury and other pollutants that make the fish from the Lumber River dangerous to eat. Some people still do eat the fish from the river but in doing so risk their own and their family's health; finding ways of educating people about the dangers of water pollution is another issue for my people.

In addition to agricultural pollutants and municipal waste plant discharges, we have a paper mill in our area. In the last 5 years, the company that runs it has been fined $850,000 for illegally running wastewater drain lines into the Lumber River. The paper industry is not the only one that does this, and this type of problem is not limited to North Carolina. It happens frequently and in many parts of the country. At the plant near my home, the illegal waste lines were well hidden, so they were used for several years before being discovered. One has to wonder about the effects on people of the chemicals that were put into the river for such a long time.

The other issue that we are facing in our area is landfill leakage. Many of the landfills in the area leak water into surrounding lands whenever it rains.

The water flowing out of the landfills gets into the subsurface water table. Many of the pollutants it carries eventually flow (both on the surface and below the surface) into area lakes and ponds and into the Lumber River, which, of course, takes the pollutants into the estuary and the ocean.

If you understand the hydrologic cycle, the nature of water pollution issues becomes clearer. The hydrologic cycle is simply the round of water evaporation, precipitation, runoff, and concentration. When it rains, the storm water runs off the land, seeking the lowest possible level. So it runs downward into pools, ponds, streams, rivers, lakes, and the ocean. Along the way to the ocean, some of it sinks down into the ground wherever it is porous. The problem of water pollution comes from the fact that anything that is not somehow fixed in place gets carried away as water runs off the land. Animal and human waste and agricultural and industrial chemicals are easily picked up and carried away by water. And, of course, most bodies of water connect with other bodies of water. So ponds feed into streams, streams into ground water and rivers, ground water into lakes and wells, rivers into lakes and the ocean. They are all connected, and whatever pollutes one is likely to eventually pollute the others. Some water is always evaporating, too. When part of a polluted body of water evaporates, most of the pollutants get left behind, which helps concentrate them. Water that evaporates drifts off to eventually condense and fall back to earth. Condensation of moisture in polluted air can cause polluted rain, as with acid rain.

A recent hurricane in my area of North Carolina dramatically demonstrated the effects of storm water runoff in spreading pollution. Because of the strength and scope of the storm, vast amounts of pesticides, farm animal waste, oil and gasoline that were on the streets, and human waste that could not be contained and treated the way it normally would be were all washed out into the rivers, the lakes, and the ocean. That pollution affected the water we drink, our land, and our food.

I mentioned oil and gas runoff above. These and other petrochemical products are a major water pollution problem. We have to produce, distribute, and store huge amounts of petrochemicals to run the machinery and systems of modern society. One of the problems that I research is petrochemical spills. When petrochemicals spill, they tend to get in the water, and when they get in the water, they can create major health problems for people. I model the extent and spread of particular chemicals within petrochemical spills. First, I try to map the spill to get an idea of how broad an area has already been contaminated. Then I create a model of how fast and in which direction or directions the spill is moving. So one of the first things that we determine is the flow direction. Then I look at which particular chemicals are in the spill and what their rate of change is to try to determine how fast they are biodegrading. Nature, over time, will take over and transform the chemicals in a spill. This is what we call biodegradation—biological alteration of the chemical pollutants. Elements are always conserved; the same is true of pollutants. So once a fuel spill has taken place, you will always have to deal with that fuel. It is never going away. You can transfer it to another place or transform it from one chemical form to another, but it will always be somewhere in some form. The value of the complicated mathematical modeling I do is that it shows where the spill has come from and how the chemicals in it have been transformed. That allows us to predict where the spill will go and what the chemicals will become in the future.

For example, with gasoline spills, the compounds that the EPA is concerned about are benzene, toulene, ethyl benzene, xylene, and methyl-tertiary-butyl-ether (MTBE). Many of these chemicals are very dangerous to human health. For instance, benzene is known to be a potent carcinogen. The last one I listed, MTBE, was developed to replace lead in gasoline to try to reduce problems that were occurring from lead pollution. But MTBE itself has turned out to be a potential major water pollutant. It metabolizes as formaldehyde in the human liver. Formaldehyde is, of course, used as a preservative and disinfectant. When it gets inside the liver, though, it can damage or destroy it and kill or cause serious illness to animals and people. Levels of MTBE ranging from 20 to 200 micrograms per liter of water have been proposed as the limit for safety, but no standard has been adopted as yet. Another thing about MTBE that makes it very dangerous is that it does not biodegrade. You can look at the level of MTBE found in a body of water or in an aquifer over a period of, say, 500 days, and there will be no change in its level.

The Lumbee community is riddled with many different types of cancer: bone, prostate, lymph, ovarian, and stomach. I would venture to say that the high levels of cancer in my community are related, as they often are, to the types of water pollution I have described here. There have been no tests done, though, to establish exactly which chemicals are causing the problems. No one has collected all of the information needed and analyzed it in the way that would answer the question of why such high rates of cancer exist among the Lumbee people. The resources have not been there, and the Lumbees have not had the power and influence to make the government pay attention to this problem. I think that this situation is all too common in Indian communities around North America.

One of the things that I want to do in this chapter is to make a suggestion for addressing the types of pollution and health problems affecting Indians that I have just described using my home area as an illustration. It is a simple suggestion: We need to bring more Native Americans into hydrology and the environmental sciences. There certainly is great impotence right now in most Indian communities concerning water pollution and other environmental issues. The communities are at the mercy of others because they lack the skilled people who can identify problems, develop solutions, and find resources to make those solutions work. I would like to see a water quality program established somewhere designed to address the needs of Indian communities.

There is a model curriculum that I have been working on entitled Environmental Control/Hazardous Waste Management. The emphasis is on water quality monitoring, and it could be a 2-year associate's degree program or could be offered as part of a 4-year degree. Initiating a program at the community college level to train water quality personnel would be a way to spearhead Indian action on water pollution problems. From there, we could try to develop specialists with even more education who might be able to get the larger society to look at water issues differently and more holistically and who might be able to promote different approaches to water that would solve some of the current problems. Perhaps the funding for such a program could come in part from water pollution fines that are assessed for polluting water that flows into Indian lands, like the $850,000 the paper company near Lumbee was fined. Funding of that sort would go a long way toward supporting Indian environmental science education and practice.

The authors in this book have said over and over again that many educated Native people feel a responsibility to their communities, an almost irresistible urge to give something back to them. That is very important to most Native people, and it certainly is true for me. It should be true for everyone, Native or not.

I read an article recently about Johnetta Cole, president of Spelman College, that may tie together all parts of my message. The article reads, "Johnetta Cole often tells the story of a young girl on the beach the morning after a storm. The beach is littered with starfish as far as she can see. Walking along, the girl stops and picks up one starfish after another and throws it back into the sea. A man stops the girl and asks what she is doing. 'The starfish will die in the hot sun unless I throw them back,' she explains. 'But there are millions of starfish here,' the man countered, 'How can you make a difference?' The little girl picks up another starfish, throws it back and says, 'It makes a difference to this one.'" I think that that is what we have to do in our efforts to support Native students, address the problems in Native communities, and deal with water issues in general. We cannot solve all of these problems all at once, but we can and must work on them one at a time with the intention of trying to "make a difference to this one."

18. Land, People, and Culture

Using Geographic Information Systems to
Build Community Capacity

First, I would like to thank the elders among us for their prayers and guidance. I am very thankful that we have elders who are meeting contemporary needs.

The section of this book under which my chapter falls is titled "The Land, the People, and Science." During the conference at which these chapters were first presented as papers, there were flags in the conference hall from various tribes around North America. These flags put the ideas for the section title into concrete form. If we look, for instance, at my tribe's flag, the Oglala Lakota flag, the tepees on it represent the communities on the homelands where my people live. They are arranged in a circle to reflect the circle of relationships and obligations among individuals and communities and the fit of both within the cycles of nature. The Oglala Lakota flag, therefore, depicts people and their relationship to communities, communities and their relationship to each other, and the relationship of all to the land. Those relationships are, for us as Native people, the foundation of our perception of ourselves and of our view of the world. Tribal flags are very important—they are graphic statements of the philosophies by which we live.

Geographic information systems (GIS) technology can also graphically depict those philosophies. My perspective in this chapter is based on my personal experiences in consulting with tribes on GIS. I entered into that field because I believe it has the potential to be of great assistance to Indian tribes in ways that fit with the cultures and places from which we come.

For 17 years I worked for IBM. I learned a lot from working for that major world corporation, which focuses on managing information with computers. But I eventually realized that working for a major corporation compromised a lot of my personal values. The company's assumptions about what Native people, in particular, need and about what is good for society, in general, did not match my beliefs. I realized that mainstream institutions and organizations still generally assume that success among Native people is hindered by their traditional cultures and that they need to shed those traditions and assimilate. I do not accept either idea.

Our ancestors were very sensitive in their relationships with the land. They systematically organized experiential information about cycles, seasons, connections, and strategies into their cultures. Experience was evolved into knowledge, and knowledge was evolved into wisdom. So I think we need to reject the notion that has been promoted by mainstream institutions, and even by some of our own people, that disconnecting ourselves from tradition, our elders, our ancestors, and their experiences will help us succeed now and in the future. These things eventually come full circle; science is finally coming around to accepting some parts of the perspective that we have had for centuries. Keith James talks in Chapter 1 about how Native traditions and some parts of science can fit well together if we as Native people learn to use science in our own ways and for purposes that fit with our own world-view and value system. Through my experiences of working with computers and geographic information systems, I have come to the same conclusion.

An example of a shift in mainstream science's perceptions is the relatively new idea of taking a long-term view of the effects of environmental exploitation. Until recently, the focus on exploitation for short-term gain has been the dominant value in mainstream society. The advent of digital data sets, geographic information, and remote sensing technologies promotes long-term perspectives by providing the ability to apply prescriptive means to a goal through analytical research. Taking the perspective of the next seven generations is a common tradition with most Aboriginal cultures. I believe that our responsibility in the present is to remember our past as we think about our future. This would apply equally to our great-great-grandchildren's future. Then, when we meet our ancestors again in the next life and shake hands with them, when they look us in the eyes, they will see that, yes, we have made the same efforts for the next seven generations that they made for us.

Geographic information systems has the potential to help us consider, all at once, traditional knowledge; scientific understanding; current issues, resources, and goals; and future obligations and possibilities. It is also compatible with presenting that information in a holistic visual format that fits with the world-view of Native people. When I recognized the potential for the amalgamation of tradition and technology, it reminded me of traditional Indian people, who knew everything about the land and how to work with it. Information about the intertwining of people and land is what should drive GIS and other spatial technologies. Combining GIS with harmonious values will assist us in understanding just how the land and the people are connected. So for me, the Indianization of GIS can help us honor our ancestors and carry on with their philosophies of understanding the interconnections of this world and the effects our current actions will have on the next seven generations.

The process of understanding the current needs of our communities has a lot to do with understanding tradition—where we come from plays an important role in where we are and where we are going. But everything hinges on gathering the right information and organizing it in the right ways. Geographic information systems can help do exactly that. My approach to developing information management for Native communities is to try to help community members understand how they can organize information using technology so that the system of information incorporates their standards, their goals, their tribal wisdom, and their point of view. I help communities do needs assessments and then help them devise implementation strategies for GIS technology that fit with their community's traditions, goals, and values. In using GIS to meet needs such as managing natural resources or providing government services to a community, we incorporate tradition and culture into the information system and all aspects of the process by which it is used.

Let me give you an example of the potential value of GIS for Native communities. I have been working for the last few years with the Squamish First Nation in British Columbia (BC). In BC there are many First Nations, and only a few had treaties with mainstream Canadian government until recently. In the United States and among the Native bands in other parts of Canada, most Indian groups with any substantial population or land claims have treaties with the federal government. The provisions of those treaties often have been forced upon them, are unfair in many respects, and may be violated sometimes, but at least something exists on paper that protects some of the tribe's rights. As Cliff Atleo explains eloquently in Chapter 23, though, almost no treaties were ever signed by the tribes in BC. The BC First Nations were simply squeezed into tiny remnants of their previous territory, and even those were unilaterally declared crown lands that ultimately belonged to the government. Indigenous people who had inhabited the land for eons found themselves residing on fragments of their traditional territories without title to that land, at the sufferance of the usurpers. Only a few years ago did the Canadian federal government and the British Columbian provincial government begin attempting to negotiate treaties with the various Native bands and First Nations in that province. Thus, the Squamish First Nation made its first entry into treaty making in modern times.

The first step the Squamish First Nation wanted to take in the treaty process was to develop maps of both their traditional territories and current community conditions. I was asked to help implement a state-of-the-art GIS technology for the Squamish chiefs to use at the treaty negotiation table. They had high expectations of sitting there with laptop computers accessing and manipulating maps that would allow them to see different land options as they discussed them with the BC provincial government. They wanted to be able to see right away the scope and meaning of verbal and legal proposals about boundaries, resources, easements, and other proposed land arrangements. They expected a lot, but their goal was very inspirational to me. The first thing we did was to create a map of their traditional territory and the pattern of use they had made of it. The boundaries of the Squamish Nation's traditional lands were defined by systematic analysis of oral histories of some of their elders, correlated with archeological and historic data in existing records about land and water areas that were associated with the tribe. The map took information about the past from documents, oral histories, and other cultural materials and linked it to current real-world coordinates in a GIS system. To me, the map set an important precedent for other Native communities. It took traditional Native knowledge and mainstream historical information and maps and linked them, using sophisticated computer and graphic-presentation technologies in a scheme of physical coordinates. The result was that the Squamish chiefs had access to tribal knowledge in a form that used the same data standards and mapping techniques as those employed by the provincial and federal governments. The Squamish leadership now accesses and uses information through the most advanced available techniques of information gathering, integration, and display. This application and use of state-of-the-art spatial technology approaches should help to make the modern treaty negotiations in British Columbia more comprehensive, equitable, and forthright.

In addition to its value for community and resource management, and for the integration of traditional knowledge with modern goals and issues (such as treaty negotiation), GIS can also play an important role in educating Native youth. Cultures and traditions are nothing except organized information. But cultural wisdom and tradition are not static. In traditional culture, information was continually updated and integrated with what was already known. I think that keeping our cultural wisdom up to date is also part of our modern responsibility. I have an obligation to pass on to the next generation and the generations beyond what I have learned and what I have discovered to be important and true. So it is critical that we think about how to incorporate new knowledge, developed from new techniques, with Native cultures as they currently stand. Information management and presentation play a critical role in this process. When it comes to education, we must carefully consider how to use technology to pass on both the refined wisdom of the past and the new discoveries of the present and future to the next seven generations. That is something I believe we really need to work on and validate in our Indian education systems.

Along the road to learning about GIS, I attended the International Cartographic Society conference at the Newberry Library in 1994. At that conference was a man named Malcolm Lewis from Sheffield, England, who had done extensive research over the course of some 20 years into Indian cartography. He had a massive collection of different types of maps created by Native individuals and groups. Some were on birch bark, some on ivory tusks, and others on hides. Discovering his collection of Indian maps was pivotal in my understanding of the potential of GIS for Native people because here was a mainstream scientist validating traditional Indian cartography. Presenting traditional maps and the ways of conceiving the world that went with them to Native children would be a compelling technique for teachers to use to introduce geography, cartography, computer graphic-spatial display techniques, as well as other aspects of science. Indian students could learn science and at the same time learn that their ancestors were skilled cartographers. The old maps could also be used to teach the history of Native contributions to what non-Natives call the "discovery" of this continent. Most people do not know, for instance, that Lewis and Clark depended on many Indian maps in their journey across the North American continent.

Another value of those old Native maps is that they show how we, as Native people, think; our minds are generally naturally inclined toward spatial cognition. The spatial views of old-time Indian groups differed, however, from the ways modern mainstream society treats space. For instance, in traditional Indian map making, the relative position and size of a feature— say, a lake—had little to do with the abstract scales or two-dimensional analog representation of three-dimensional space used in non-Native maps. Instead, it had more to do with the importance of each feature as a resource—say, for food—and with whether it was a sacred site. I think it would be worthwhile to do some systematic research and analysis of the principles of Native cartography. It could be an effective tool for helping Native and non-Native people understand how Indian cultures traditionally organized their views of the physical world. We could learn more about the differences and similarities of the world-views of different Indian groups and learn more about patterns of thinking that still, to some extent, influence the minds of Indian people today. Research on Indian cartography could provide inspiration to Native youth and might also aid in understanding how best to structure information for effective Indian education.

Another important issue about information technology was brought to my attention by Andrew Bear Robe. Andrew is a friend of mine from the Siksika First Nation in Alberta, Canada. He pointed out to me that the use of computers could potentially be altering the brain and mental processes of humans. I have given considerable thought to this idea and believe that we may need to consider how computers may alter the organization and function of our minds, especially the minds of our offspring. For example, I have children who, from early life, have had computers and computer games that respond to their commands instantly and without complaint. Without the proper guidance and experience, they might easily have come to expect instant gratification from life, in general. People whose minds have been strongly influenced by interaction with artificial intelligence can end up wanting and expecting everything to happen right away, and they can have trouble understanding patterns of information that unfold slowly or goals that need to be pursued long-term. Educators often promote technology as the solution to educational problems, when in reality we have to realize that computers are just tools that need to be used appropriately and made to work effectively with other tools. Our primary goals for education still need to be the development of the brain capacity of our children and students' understanding of where their capabilities fit within the cultural and environmental context. These are the types of things we need to consider when deciding how to use technology or how to educate our children with it and about it.

Science is nothing more than quantified, systematized information. Native people may have some unique information that will take science in new directions. The information that we hold in our cultures and traditions was developed over time through observation and experience. Our information also comes from another source: the spiritual knowledge we receive from dreams and visions and from our connections to the earth that are built into all aspects of our cultures. I hope and believe that we can communicate some of that knowledge to ourselves, to others, and to future generations through information technology. We can make contributions to science and to the general well-being of the earth, while at the same time strengthening and validating our own systems of culture (information management), just as our ancestors used to do.

Those are the experiences and ideas I wanted to share with you. The things I just mentioned are not solely my ideas. They came from my interactions with many other people who I have visited with and talked to through the years, and I acknowledge their help and guidance. My work has taken me all over North America, and I am always very grateful to meet and learn from Indian people and to see the common threads that we all share when we seek to understand the land, the people, and science.

Jane Mt. Pleasant

19. The Three Sisters

Care for the Land and the People

I am going to talk about agriculture in this chapter, and I always like to start by giving a little bit of background about myself and a little bit about the context of my work in agriculture. I think certainly my feelings about corn are both heretical and intuitive. For many years when I have entered a cornfield, I have known that I was walking among conscious living things— entities that were surely more than just plants. As an agronomist at a major land-grant university, that is certainly not something I readily reveal to my colleagues, students, or even to the farmers with whom I work. But I know that these feelings are rooted in an understanding of the natural world and of corn that extends back generations and reflects knowledge from another vantage point, a Native perspective. The cornfield as a place where science and Native culture meet is a metaphor for my life as I struggle to find my place and manage the tension between Western science and my Indian roots. I love working with corn, and as an agronomist I am in awe of its productivity. But I also know that it represents much more than a prolific agricultural crop. It is an enormous gift to human beings and speaks of life and connection to the earth in ways that are profoundly simple and complex at the same time. This struggle between indigenous and scientific knowledge also speaks to the theme of this book: using science, math, and technology to serve the needs of Native communities. Agricultural science can serve Native communities, but engaging science and culture is neither straightforward nor easy.

My own involvement with agriculture was an unplanned event. I ended up enmeshed with corn after driving a cab for almost 8 years in New York City. My father was Tuscarora. He was raised on the Tuscarora reservation just north of Buffalo, New York. He left the reservation when he was 17, at the beginning of the Depression, and never lived there again after that. With no resources and intense determination, the details of which I know very little, he graduated from Fredonia State College in New York and became an elementary school teacher for the Onondaga Nation in Syracuse and later principal of a Hopi school in Arizona. World War II disrupted his teaching career. He became a foreman for a pharmaceutical company in New York and continued with that until he retired. He was married first to an Onondaga woman, who died. They had two children, my half-siblings, both of whom are Onondaga. He later married my mother, a non-Indian, and had four more children of whom I am the youngest.

I grew up in a household in which my Tuscarora heritage was acknowledged but seldom examined. My connection to my extended family at the reservation was tenuous and disjointed. Growing up in a middle-class suburb outside of Syracuse, I was expected to go to college, but I was not expected to maintain, much less strengthen, any connection with my Native heritage. I did not follow that path. After attending college for one term, I dropped out and moved to New York City and became a taxi driver. After several years of driving a cab, I knew it was time to move on and find a new career.

A trip to the library turned up soil mapping as my new profession, and I started on a path that led me simultaneously to a career as an agronomist and to a deepening connection with my Native roots. My return to college at Cornell University was the first step in my plan to become a soil mapper and to work for the Soil Conservation Service. But once at Cornell, I was quickly waylaid. In retrospect, it seems almost planned. In the summer following my first year at Cornell, funding for a summer apprenticeship with the Soil Conservation Service fell through at the last minute, and I ended up working for my Cornell faculty advisor, a soil scientist who conducted field research on corn. By the end of the summer, I knew that I wanted to work with plants. I felt this intense pleasure with corn that was both wonderful and disconcerting. That attraction to corn pulled me relentlessly through a bachelor's degree, a master's degree, and a doctorate, and it has led me back to Cornell in a faculty position where I was asked to conduct research on sustainable soil and crop management. I focused on corn systems. It wasn't until I returned to Cornell as a faculty member that I began to understand that experience more fully.

There was tension between my training as a scientist and my roots in a culture that is based on corn. I knew that I loved working with corn, watching it grow, and handling the ears. I was passionately involved with researching ways to grow it more sustainedly, but I saw little connection between my life as a scientist and my identity as a Tuscarora. Shortly after I joined the faculty at Cornell, the American Indian Program asked me to oversee and coordinate the program's emerging agriculture projects. At that point, I began to sense the complexities of this issue. The agriculture project was charged with growing a traditional Iroquois white flour corn that was in danger of being lost because few Indians were planting it.

Almost immediately I was expected to be the expert in Iroquois agriculture and crops. In ignorance, I headed to the library and discovered corn anew from a different vantage point. I read descriptions of Iroquois agriculture as it was practiced at the time of first contact and found a body of knowledge about agriculture and its role in the Iroquois Confederacy that had been completely invisible to me. Through my historical reading, I discovered the Three Sisters system of agriculture. In a Three Sisters garden, you plant corn, beans, and squash together in hills.

Many people believe that the northeast Indians in general and the Iroquois in particular were primarily a primitive hunting and gathering people. They think that if you had come into New York State in the late 1500s, you would have encountered a landscape that was wilderness, completely forested, and showing little human impact on the landscape. But the truth is much different. The Iroquois were primarily farmers, and their agriculture was very productive. The strength of the Iroquois Confederacy, in fact, came in large part from that very productive and vibrant agricultural base. If you had been in what is now central New York State in the late 1500s, you would have encountered people engaged in rather intense and very large-scale agriculture, not backyard gardening. Many times when I talk about this, particularly to school groups, the children just look at me and say, "This is not what we know about Iroquois people. Where did this information come from?" Surprisingly, most of the information that I have gathered about traditional Iroquois agriculture has come from the journals, the diaries, and the reports of the European explorers and military leaders.

For example, in 1535 Jacques Cartier, as he traveled down the Saint Lawrence River, made the earliest reference to Iroquois agriculture that I was able to find. He described in his journal passing village after village of Indian people. Surrounding the villages were large fields of corn, large extensive fields of corn, and within the villages themselves were large granaries where the corn was stored. About 100 years later, a Dutch explorer, Arendt van Colaer, coming up the Hudson River described a scene almost exactly in those same words. I also read journal entries written by soldiers in General

Sullivan's campaign as they pillaged their way through central New York in the late 1700s in an attempt to wipe out the Iroquois Confederacy. They described in stunning detail a vibrant and dynamic agriculture that provided a stable and very comfortable standard of living for Iroquois people, far better than what most European colonists enjoyed at that time.

Certainly, when the Europeans arrived in the northeast, the agriculture they encountered was very different from what they knew. It was different in two primary ways. First, the primary crop that the Iroquois were growing was corn. This was a crop that the Europeans had not seen before. They were planting small grains such as barley, oats, wheat, and rye. Second, what was striking to them was the fact that Iroquois were planting without tillage. They had no draft animals and no plows. Again, this was very striking because the Europeans at that time were using draft animals to plow. They were tilling the land, and then they would broadcast, meaning that they would scatter their seeds out onto the tilled ground after they had plowed it. When they came to the northeast, they brought their seeds but left their plows and their draft animals at home. Their first attempts at agriculture were complete failures. They tried to sow their oats, wheat, and rye onto unplowed ground, and it was a complete disaster. They got no yield at all. So they began to look a little bit more closely at the cropping system the Native peoples were using.

When I used my training as an agricultural scientist to analyze the Three Sisters cropping system, I was jolted to find that it embodied all the concepts and principles needed for successful corn growth. Beans, because they are legumes, add nitrogen to the soil that the other two plants need. In other words, they add free fertilizer. The corn, in turn, provides physical support for the beans. The Iroquois used pole beans, and if you have ever grown them in your garden, you know that you are supposed to put in a pole for each one of those bean plants to twine up around. In this particular system, you do not need to add poles; the corn plant provides it as it grows. Now the squash, because it grows low to the ground and has very big leaves, reduces the ability of weeds to grow and interfere with the food crops. Finally, the three crops eaten together provide a very balanced diet of vitamins, minerals, carbohydrates, and the full complement of amino acids for protein.

Agronomists also now know that there are a lot of good reasons for planting on mounds. First, it is a handy way to control plant populations. Corn is very sensitive to population, and a very easy way to control the number of plants per field is to simply limit the number that you plant per mound. Also, because planting in mounds does not involve tillage, it is excellent for preventing soil erosion. It also is an excellent way to improve the soil's physical composition; all of the plant residues from the corn and any weeds when they die become concentrated in the mound, and the organic matter improves the soil. Mound planting also concentrates and recycles nutrients. Corn has to have nutrients to grow, and Iroquois people did not have access to inorganic fertilizers at a feed and fertilizer store. They had to rely on the recycling of organic nutrients. The Three Sisters system does this very nicely. As Freda Porter-Locklear points out in Chapter 17, water quality might be better if modern farmers made less use of inorganic fertilizers. Finally, mound planting facilitates weed control. Weed spread is reduced by gaps between mounds, and it is much easier to deal with weeds in one hill at a time rather than weeds that spread across an entire field. Though developed by people with no science training, the Three Sisters system of the Iroquois was mimicked by mainstream farmers and studied by mainstream scientists. It made an enormous contribution to modern agriculture but has been almost completely forgotten.

Natural sciences, particularly the plant sciences, can be used to engage Native youth in educational pursuits that have enormous relevance for Indian people. Understanding the science-based principles for resource management will allow Indian nations to effectively manage their own forest, fish, wildlife, and agricultural and mineral resources. On the other hand, understanding traditional Indian approaches to natural resources has value for both Native and non-Native people. Traditional knowledge has enabled Native communities to practice sustainable resource management for centuries. Indian people must be able to engage Western science on its own terms to deal effectively with non-Indians who recognize knowledge only from their own narrow vantage point.

Many Native youth are rapidly losing touch with the natural world. Their estrangement from the earth and its plant and animal life must be reversed if the Native nations are to survive and to flourish. For Iroquois people, in particular, I believe that losing the ability and the desire to grow corn sustainedly threatens our cultural identity and political and economic survival.

Agricultural science can also be used to help in the conservation of traditional crops and biodiversity. Our agricultural project at Cornell University grows Iroquois flour corn and distributes it to Native gardeners and farmers across our region. We also sell or give away food corn for long house ceremonies, community events, and entrepreneurial activities on reservation communities. Replicated field experiments on the Three Sisters contribute to our understanding of these cropping systems but also affirm the value and knowledge embedded in these agricultural systems; in this way, traditional knowledge gains credibility.

There are some very specific ways that agricultural science and agricultural education can serve Native communities. They can connect Native youth and adults to their agricultural roots and remind them of the enormous gift that their ancestors have given all people. For Native youth, a garden of traditional plants is a very powerful way to connect science with culture. First, it introduces science concepts and issues such as nutrient cycling, biodiversity, and plant competition that can have immediate relevance and attraction for young people. A garden is a living botany lesson that can be touched, smelled, and tasted. At the very minimum, it teaches plant anatomy, plant physiology, and ecology. At the same time, a garden allows young people to connect in multiple ways with the culture of traditional agricultural practices and their place in Native life.

Caring for corn, for instance, demands a relationship with the earth. You cannot help but watch in awe as a corn plant emerges from the soil, unfolding its leaves and reaching for the sky. Successful corn production depends upon a delicate balance between soil, plant, and atmosphere, but it also requires the knowledgeable and respectful participation of human beings. Corn will not survive without people to plant, tend, and harvest it. Growing corn demonstrates the complexity of life, an intertwining web that connects all living and nonliving elements on our planet. Working with corn can change the world-view of Native youth.

I want to briefly discuss some of the specific activities that I have used to educate both Native and non-Native youth about plant science. Many students have little understanding of where food comes from. In the "Grind Away" program, I bring into a classroom a whole living corn plant with an ear on it and let the students thoroughly examine it. At the same time, I also have available ears of corn on which the corn kernels are dry. I ask the students to remove the kernels from the cob. We then grind them in a mill. The students are encouraged to smell and touch the freshly ground corn. Finally, we use the ground corn to make corn muffins, corn bread, or tortillas. So the students have a chance to see, from the very beginning, how the corn plant has given us this food.

I also have another activity called "Corn, the Amaizing Grain" ("amaizing" as in maize), which demonstrates all the different ways we use corn in the world's food supply. We assemble a variety of food products that use corn directly, such as corn meal, tortillas, cornstarch, baby food, soda, and oil. I ask students to examine the ingredient list and find corn in each product. We then talk about the indirect use of corn, that is, its use after it has been fed to animals who are then used in the production of milk, hamburger, ice cream, fried chicken, and other animal or animal by-product foods. Making the connection between corn fed to animals and the animal products we consume is particularly valuable for younger children. We also talk about how corn is used in the production of some fabrics and some chemicals that are widely used.

One of my favorite exercises is to have students plant a Three Sisters garden based on the agricultural system used by the Iroquois in the northeast for several hundred years. Examining the system offers many opportunities for students to learn about plant biology, intercropping, nutrient cycling, and sustainability in agriculture. I ask students to note the similarities and differences in the parts of the three types of plants. You can also consider planting each of these crops in separate fields (monoculture) in order to have a comparison point for the Three Sisters approach (a form of polyculture). Students can then see for themselves the advantages and disadvantages of each approach. You can, for example, look at which system produces more— that is, have students calculate yield from each type of garden. They learn that the Three Sisters approach generally produces more, and we discuss what role each plant plays in the polycultural system.

Other activities I use that I will not describe in detail are the corn relay race; a comparison of the amounts of rice, corn, beef, wheat, and potatoes consumed worldwide annually; and the dissection of a kernel of corn to demonstrate the botanical makeup of a seed. A final example of an activity that I like very much is one that I call "Using the Three Sisters to Explode Myths." Examining myths about indigenous peoples and their agriculture is a positive learning experience for both Native and non-Native students. Drawing on the types of historical documents I mentioned earlier and using principles of Western science, we can present students with a much better picture of Native people and our traditional place in the world than what they have previously encountered in books, on television, or in movies.

Many people, after they hear me talk about the Three Sisters, say, "Listen, this is great, but what is the relevance? Why would we be the least bit interested in the Three Sisters in the 21st Century?" My answer is that there are two reasons. The first is simply that corn is immensely important to our lives now, and it is important that everyone remember that it was Native people, primarily Native women farmers and plant breeders, who gave them that gift. The second reason is that the Three Sisters technique is a model for thinking about and creating sustainability. There are many people in the agricultural community—farmers, researchers such as myself, other people involved in agriculture in any way—who worry about the sustainability of our agricultural system. Their concerns include the fact that our modern agriculture is very dependent on finite oil reserves. What will we do when we run out of oil to produce the fertilizer and pesticides on which our agriculture depends so heavily, or what if the price of oil suddenly increases substantially again, as it did in the 1970s? There is also the concern about the very large problem of soil erosion in modern industrial farming. The topsoil, the most fertile part, is lost first to erosion from our fields; this has a great impact on the productivity of farms and seems to be on the increase. As Freda Porter-Locklear describes, when those soils erode, they also carry agricultural chemicals, fertilizers, and pesticides with them into the water we depend on and into the air we breathe. So our surface waters and our ground water become contaminated by the leaching of nitrates and pesticides. We have clear evidence that the health of wildlife has been negatively affected by this. Why is it likely to be different for people? Many are also concerned about food safety. Modern industrial agriculture makes heavy use of pesticides, and we really do not know what the long-term effects might be of eating foods that have been treated with those pesticides. Finally, there is also a great deal of concern about the loss of diversity in our crops. As agricultural specialization intensifies, the number of crops and the number of varieties of those crops decrease. When diversity is low, a sudden disease that strongly affects one of the few varieties could potentially cut food availability drastically. The number of crops on which we currently depend is perilously small, and many agricultural scientists are very concerned about this.

Going back to the Three Sisters, the thing that strikes me about it is that it is highly productive without artificial fertilizers, without pesticides, and without tillage. Ask a farmer today to grow corn without one of those aids and he will tell you that it cannot be done. Many farmers today understand how to grow corn without using artificial fertilizers; simply put the corn in rotation with a legume, such as alfalfa. Ask him to grow corn without two of these three standard approaches, let us say no tillage and no fertilizer, and some could do it, but they would find it hard and would probably suffer some decline in output. If you asked farmers or agricultural scientists to grow corn without tillage, fertilizers, or any pesticides, the great majority would tell you that it simply could not be done. Yet, we know that the Iroquois Confederacy thrived for several hundred years based on an agricultural system that used none of the pillars of modern agriculture.

I think we can learn a tremendous amount from the Three Sisters system. I am not saying that all of our farmers should begin using the Three Sisters approach, but I do think that there is plenty we can learn from the philosophy behind it. It is basically a philosophy that says we need to think about maintaining a balance in the resource base, a balance between what our way of life contributes to the earth and the things that we take from the earth. Iroquois people have always known that this balance is crucial to the health of both people and the earth. It is very much what we consider a basis for our philosophy of life; as Jhon Goes in Center and others have argued, one must plan for the seventh generation and live in a way that will allow it to survive. The Three Sisters system is a model for thinking about and living that philosophy. It also certainly can provide a way of engaging our young people in thinking about all of the impacts that our human systems—our agricultural systems, our community systems, and our scientific and economic systems—are having on our world. Only by truly understanding those impacts can we plan for that seventh generation.

As I told you, I dearly love corn. One spring morning during the period when I was learning about the history of Iroquois agriculture, I was planting corn in mounds for a Three Sisters field experiment. Suddenly, I was struck by the realization that Iroquois women had been planting corn continuously in my region of the world for more than 800 years. At that moment, I very consciously joined the ranks of generations of Native women who have planted corn to sustain life. That revelation has powerfully affected my life. I now have this glimmer of understanding of what it means to honor the earth and to take my place among Iroquois women who love corn. When I enter the cornfield today, I feel the corn spirit. Science and spirit engage in my life in ways that are ultimately enriching and challenging. I feel the tension of this conflict on a very personal level, and I am convinced that science can serve Native peoples in very specific and productive ways.

I really think that, if Native people fail to grow corn, we will lose some things that cannot be replaced. I hope that we can persuade our young people that agriculture has a great deal of value and meaning for us all. I believe that getting more young Native people involved in learning and living traditional agricultural philosophies will make a great difference in their lives, will make a great difference in the continuation of Native cultures, and will make a great difference in the health of the earth for the seventh generation.

Part 5

Science and Self-Governance

Keith James

20. Science and Self-Governance

Power, Practice, and Politics

Remember, there is nothing that we can do except to help you to realize your own dreams. So I say to every tribal leader here, we must share the vision, and it must be fundamentally yours—for your children and their future. If you will give us that vision . . . we will achieve it.–President Bill Clinton in a speech at Pine Ridge Reservation, 1999

As I noted in Chapter 1, all of the issues covered in this book are affected by governance and leadership, and all of them in turn affect the quality of leadership and governance. Lack of leadership, lack of accountability, and lack of coordination have several times contributed to the undoing of Indian communities and their goals. Thus, tribal stability and advancement necessitates programs and strategies for promoting effective leadership and governance, along with visions and plans to energize and guide future action. Strategic planning is needed that leads to formal and workable policies for entrepreneurial activity, infrastructure development, educational improvement, and environmental management.

The governance system in most reservation or reserve communities was imposed by force by Europeans and remains in conflict with cultural principles, community expectations and desires, and practical necessities. Many elders believe their roles have been extinguished; relinquishment of decision making to politicians has created confusion and discord; current systems and external manipulations have created family and factional divisions that prevent effective action. The infighting and politicized decision making in Indian communities make some people feel that those with useful skills and knowledge tend to be ignored because effectiveness is really not the main priority driving the decision-making process. One highly educated and skilled conference participant, for instance, whose community was experiencing a bout of strong turmoil, talked during informal sessions about his recent decision to look for a new position because of the frustration and stress the community situation had created for him. Finally, related communities have been separated by mainstream government policies, and collaborations across Native communities have been greatly hindered by mainstream regulations, decisions, and divide-and-conquer strategies.

How do we create better governance and leadership? How do we reconcile culturally traditional roles, dynamics, and processes with the new demands of the modern world? Reggie Crowshoe argues that we must begin by re-vitalizing tribal traditions, then move on to systematically integrating those traditions with modern goals and needs, and complete the process by devising ways of mediating between tradition-based tribal governance and the external structures and processes of the larger society. He describes the mechanisms for and successes at achieving these ends on his own Canadian First Nation's reserve as an example for other Native communities. His experience links governance systems and practices with several issues in the culture, health, and education sections of this book. It also demonstrates how Indian leader-ship programs at the college level can be instrumental in reconceptualizing and rebuilding tribal governance systems.

George Thomas grapples with some key issues in his chapter. How do we get tribal government leaders, elders, and grass-roots community groups to connect, cooperate, and act in concert? What are the communication, decision-making, planning, management, organizational, and other skills re-quired for effective leadership in Native communities? Can scientific training contribute to those skills, and how can effective leadership contribute to promoting education, community and economic development, community health, and tribal culture? Where is local action required, and where would collaboration among the leaders of different Native communities be benefi-cial? Thomas's call for shared visions across tribal boundaries and for better intertribal planning and programming to execute such shared visions is sup-ported with facts and is compellingly presented. He discusses why it is difficult for any single tribe to address its most pressing problems alone. He argues that if traditional alliances can be rebuilt and promoted then community, cultural, and economic renewal are possible and Native self-sufficiency is attainable. He argues that strong, stable national (and international) united Native forums and organizations would be instrumental in preserving and advancing local Indian communities. His discussion strongly links governance issues to science and technology education for Indians and also to Indian community and economic development. While looking at intertribal collaboration, Thomas introduces an issue that has been the subject of substantial debate among Indian peoples. Some believe that relatively small bands or community groups were the prime unit of governance in most traditional tribal societies. Others argue either that alliances among bands and communities were widespread and critical to traditional governance or that the demands of the modern world necessitated broad alliances and unified action regardless of what might be traditional. Reggie Crowshoe's presentation includes some description of historic links between the governance systems within and across communities that may help reconcile the two perspectives. Both Thomas and Cliff Atleo also propose combining both approaches when appropriate for particular goals or needs.

Cliff Atleo's chapter complements the others in this section in several ways. He relates how both the traditional and the Western-based knowledge of the members of his community have been brought to bear in a coordinated way for effective environmental management. In addition, he discusses how a regional intertribal collaboration was combined with strategies for effectively using mainstream governance systems and for building coalitions with mainstream allies to create the leverage needed to initiate a power-sharing arrangement with the British Columbian provincial government. Atleo's presentation joins strategies and systems for gaining and using power with his tribe's culture, economics, and environmental management needs. He also persuasively argues for and vividly demonstrates the potential value to Native people of sharing information and coordinating efforts across the artificial borders of the three mainstream nations of North America. Promoting such international exchange and collaboration was a major motivation for producing this book.

Some have described Indians as being generally more group connected than North Americans of European descent. This may be true in some respects, but it is also a stereotype of limited accuracy. Some of the tribes most renowned for their strategic and fighting ability in war, for instance, also have traditions in which warriors must agree to fight. They did not fight to avoid punishment by their kind or because of any blind obedience to one person or system. They had to agree, instead, that *this* fight at *this* time was one that *they* and their families needed to help make.

The root of effective governance for tribes, then, is the ability to sway individuals and family groups with a compelling vision. That vision can come from an individual or from a group and can be implemented through verbal persuasion, by spiritual means, by logical means, by means of a call to honor, or by means of emotional ties. If one person tends more toward spiritual guidance and I want her agreement, the question is whether I can muster enough spiritual power to move her. If another tends more toward ties of emotion and duty and I want his agreement, can I create or call upon the appropriate ties? The same is true if we are trying to elicit unified action within a tribe or across groups of tribes. Tribes and communities each have their own unique tendencies—shaped by varied traditions, systems, internal relations, and situations—toward certain types of motivations that will most effectively move them. Creating the types of common actions and building the shared structures that are needed will take strategic and tactical leverage that can counter the centrifugal forces from within and from external governments (federal, state, or provincial) and mainstream society. The techniques and tactics employed will need to differ somewhat to match the balance of tendencies in, and influences on, each of the groups whose agreement is sought.

Ultimately, Indian survival and success may well rest on the question of whether the proper balance and strength of approaches can be found. The authors in this section argue that they can, and they provide guidance to paths leading to a place of vision, balance, and strength.

Reggie Crowshoe

21. Rebuilding Tradition to Create Workable Modern Systems and Practices for Indian Communities

I am from the Blackfoot Nation on the Peigan Reserve in southern Alberta, Canada. We are one of five tribes in southern Alberta that signed Treaty Number 7 with what was then the British government in Canada. The greater Blackfoot Nation consists of my Blackfoot Nation, the Blood tribe in Alberta, and the Blackfeet in northern Montana.

I want to tell you, from a Canadian First Nation's perspective, about finding approaches in tradition to solve modern problems. My background is largely in the ceremonies and traditional culture of our Blackfoot people. My first language is Blackfoot, and my thought processes are pretty well rooted within the Blackfoot ceremonial concepts. I have also, however, gone to Western schools and recently went to the University of Lethbridge to work with Leroy Littlebear and to obtain a degree in business administration. Leroy has been working with the communities on the Peigan Reserve to rework our systems back toward traditional ways. The information given here is based on the research we did on traditional Blackfoot philosophy and practices to extract processes and to develop workable systems that could be used to deal with current community issues and needs.

The federal government in Canada has been in the process of turning control of some social service systems back to the local Indian communities; health service delivery is one example. One of the problems with our taking control of those systems is that the federal government built them based on processes and approaches—the hierarchic structure is one example—that are not traditional to Blackfoot people. Consequently, those systems have never really worked in our communities. Since they did not come from our community and were imposed upon us, my people do not respect them or want to use them. So when the government had meetings to discuss their turning over control of community services, few people from the community attended.

Another area in which we need a process to bridge Blackfoot tradition and Western systems and approaches is in dealing with private corporations. A lot of corporations come to the Peigan Reserve and want to do business there. It could be a utility company, a petroleum company, or some other type of company; they come wanting to develop some resources or build some facility. Those corporations have Western world-views and have built their systems, structures, and practices based on that world-view. When they espouse partnership, they have a culturally based idea of what that means. Therefore, the goals and systems it involves often do not fit with how we see things. Our challenge, then, is to find a way to take Western goals, perspectives, and systems and match them with the issues and ways of our Native communities so that the partnership might be successful.

To deal with that problem on the Peigan Reserve, the tribal leadership and Leroy got together with our elders and our traditional thinkers to try to devise approaches to helping our young people become confident individuals and to building confident communities that would be able to succeed within the larger Canadian society. The elders said, "Well, we've got to extract approaches and tools from our traditional philosophy and processes, because only a system that originates from our belief system, our world-view, will work for us." The elders told us that at the turn of the century, when colonization and assimilation of our people began, the colonizers first tried to eliminate our decision-making and governance practices. The elders said, "We've had a cultural void since the turn of the century. We have lost our ceremonies and ceremonialists and the meaning and use of our traditional bundles and societies. That was all lost, and all that survived were our general cultural values and norms."

The elders told us that we cannot just take a Western approach to an issue and try to fit it with our general traditional world-view. Instead, they said, we needed to look at parallels between the specific systems and processes of Western society and those of our tradition. Only then would we be able to move ahead effectively. So with our elders, we started looking at how can we start bringing traditional practices back to our community. One of the challenges was to look at things in our language in order to capture our traditional thought processes and then translate them into English so that we could fit them with modern strategies and needs. At the same time, when we looked at Western concepts, practices, and perspectives, we had to translate them into our language so that our elders could consider their fit within our traditions.

We started the process by building a database of traditional practices using oral histories, written records, pictures, and artifacts. We used this database as a starting point for addressing our tribe's current needs. I think the first written record about the Peigans is from about 1691, written by a fur trader by the name of Calsey, who was with the American Fur Trading Company. In eastern Canada and Newfoundland, some tribes had already disappeared or were already disappearing by 1691. So we had pretty late contact with non-Natives. We looked at a number of reports from archaeologists, anthropologists, explorers, missionaries, government officials, and other professionals who wrote about our communities from 1691 through 1930. In addition to examining written records, we studied paintings and photographs that dated back to about 1840. We also incorporated oral histories from our elders about such things as ceremonies, family lineages, clan and society obligations, geographical boundaries, and materials and material use. We also looked at our traditional winter accounts that date back to the mid-1700s, at tepee designs, and at the designs of any other traditional artifacts that we could find.

We took all of this data back to the elders to extract information about our traditions and practices. We still have many ceremonialists who can take cultural material and put it right back into the context and systems in which it was originally used. The wealth of information we gathered allowed our elders to reconstitute the ceremonies and systems that had been suppressed in the early 1900s.

For example, almost every year sun dances were recorded in our winter accounts, and we wondered why. The elders explained that the sun dances brought all the different clans and tribes together. When they broke away from the large sun dance gathering, each individual community went back to its own geographical area. At the sun dance, they would have ceremonial religious activities, but it was also a way of putting into effect the mechanisms of tribal unity and decision making; the clans and tribes talked about how they had survived as a people in the past and about what they needed to do to survive in the future. Each community received beaver bundles before leaving the sun dance. The bundles were opened during ceremonies in the spring after the ice thawed and in the fall before the rivers froze. They were used to decide whether a community moved or whether it stayed at one location and to make other decisions about everyday survival. So the bundles were a legislative equivalent. Thus, the sun dances that are recorded in the winter accounts point to important processes of tribal governance.

Tepee designs provide another example of how we studied our historical traditions so that we could adapt them to modern times. Tepee designs helped us understand the traditional mechanisms of clan or medicine society membership, intellectual property ownership, and ownership transfer. Designs were very important as an expression of clan and society memberships and because of that, of rights and duties within the community. As a result, they were regulated, and nobody could own somebody else's design without going through an official purchase and a transfer ceremony. This gave us a sense of the authority that traditionally came with these designs, an understanding of the traditional concept of ownership, and information about our tribes' traditional equivalents of copyright laws and copyright transfer.

As an example of what we learned from oral history, in Blackfoot culture we have "Naupey's stories." The Naupey was a person who could talk to all of the animals and who had been part of creating the world. The Naupey stories gave us the places where, and the norms, standards, and laws by which, our people lived before contact. They are particularly useful for determining traditional boundaries and land uses when we are negotiating land claims. The stories, when we combined them with other cultural materials, were also helpful in understanding other things. They tell, for instance, about the original meaning of traditional bundles and ceremonies; how groups of people were organized to address different needs of the community; as well as about the procedures that were used to deal with each community need. We used concept mapping from the stories to figure out relationships among different bundles and societies within our communities. For instance, in looking at the concept of health, we asked which bundles were part of traditional health systems, what were the protocols for how each was involved, and what were the processes that tied them together in dealing with health?

We also located and used a number of artifacts, such as bundles and clothing, from the Peigan Reserve. We were able to retrieve our artifacts from museums and other non-Native institutions and use them to look at how social controls and social services operated before the Canadian government took them over. For instance, then as now, there was a need for a way to settle conflicts between individuals, between Indian families and the larger community, and even between communities. The Thunder Medicine bundles and the ceremonies surrounding them filled that role for us in the past, and we have adapted them to deal with conflicts in the present. This is the equivalent of the judiciary in the Canadian provincial and federal governments.

We also connected the Western concepts of mission statements, goals, and objectives of an organization to the concept of our bundles. Bundles were community property and were related to different areas of social control and social services in our community. Each bundle and the rituals around it set the rules for decision making in a particular area, for participation within a given circle structure, and for achieving some end necessary to the survival and well-being of the people. We found that bundle keepers or ceremonialists were like the managers or executives who see that goals and mission statements are generated and followed.

In mainstream Canadian society, different government agencies play important roles in delivering social programs and services. Our traditional special societies played a similar role. There was the Mucteek Society, which was a warrior society, and the Old Blows, the Horn Society, the Brave Dog Society, and the Kitfoxes, among others. Each society had its own ceremonies, which we looked at to see how they met community needs. For example, the Brave Dogs were the equivalent of the police. The Bumble Bee Society was a sort of social welfare agency, providing for those too sick, too young, too old, or too different minded to care for themselves. The Small Bird Society provided education. So these societies played administrative and social service roles. Rituals and tools also were related to social services in the community. In the Black Tail Deer dance, for example, healing society members gathered curing herbs. The Feather Game and other games provided recreation, and there was a variety of medicinal and personal curing bundles. All of those practices and processes were part of the traditional social structure that we studied so that we could rebuild community services and systems. We tried to extract the community-function aspects of the sun dance, the bundles, the societies, the dances, and the ceremonies without intruding on any sacred secrets. What we wanted were basic concepts, processes, and structures that would help our modern communities function effectively.

Another thing we looked at was the traditional system of running meetings; that system paralleled the structure of the tepee. The floor plans of our tepees are circular, so when we sat to make a decision, we traditionally sat and deliberated in a circle. Then we looked at the traditional process of reaching a decision. For instance, in Western society, certain meetings might be limited to only agency members, or they might be opened to the general public; a gavel might be used by a chairman to start a meeting. In our traditional meetings, anybody could participate. As in public meetings in Western tradition, when people first arrived at Blackfoot meetings they could talk about different things unrelated to the meeting topic. Once the ceremonialist put the smudge on an altar inside of the circle, however, the side discussions ceased and everybody focused on the topic of the gathering.

The pipe was very important to decision making since it sanctified the discussion. For example, somebody might say to the tribal leaders, "George stole my horse." The leaders could ask George if he stole the horse, but he was not obliged to answer. Yet, if a ceremonialist offered him the pipe and he smoked it, he was giving his oath that he did not steal the horse, and the discussion would be over. If he did not smoke the pipe, then he had to pay for the horse. He would know that the pipe was so respected that if he were found to have used it dishonestly the people would banish him from the community. So the pipe provided a context and mechanism for gathering facts and reaching judgments. The pipe acted as a sort of legal seal on discussions.

The figure below gives an example of how we tried to use all of the information we gathered from the different sources I discussed above to address practical issues. The figure shows our administrative, decision-making, and service delivery systems for health care. We recognized the need to use the basic tepee floor plan to structure our systems. We then incorporated roles that were equivalent to those of the different bundle keepers who were traditionally involved in the areas of individual and community health, plus those who were involved in the areas of traditional administration and decision making. We also added versions of the altar-and-smudge and pipe ceremonies to organize the process of health planning, decision making, and service provision.

Within the tepee structure shown in the figure, many roles and departments are arranged in a particular pattern. In our tepee structure, the females sit on one side and the males sit on the other side. The female role is really to provide the mandate for the group, because traditionally the women, not the men, physically handled the bundles. Women, in other words, were responsible for consensus building, and men were responsible for putting that consensus into action. We, therefore, also divide our current systems, our modern management circles, along the lines of those different gender roles. The titles of all of the different tribal departments and directors (e.g., social

Peigan Nation Health Services Structure

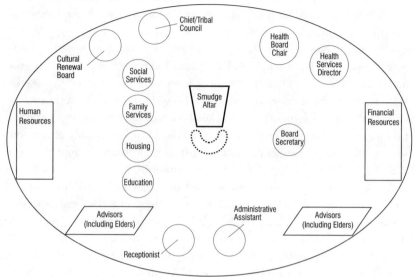

services, health services, housing, and education) are translations of the titles of the various ceremonialists who carried the different bundles (mandates) and were in charge of seeing that they were used properly. Traditionally, the ceremonialists looked after the community, and that is what our current department heads and directors do now, using means that merge traditional approaches with modern necessities and techniques.

For example, one community service that we have rebuilt along traditional lines is education. Incorporating traditional practices, roles, and structures into education has helped our people, especially our young people, better understand their traditions and themselves. One of the things that the elders talked about when we started this project was how we were losing our young people at a very high rate. They were dying off as fast as the elders. Our elders said that we need a bridge to tradition for our young people so that they will have greater confidence in themselves and a firm base on which to build. The community asked, "Can we look at creating traditional conflict resolution systems in each local school?" and "Can we teach our language by using the information on traditional practices and roles that you have developed?" We have begun doing both, and this has helped create confident, grounded young people who are now not only doing better in school but are also living longer and succeeding better in life.

We have been told that we Blackfoot Peigans missed out on the industrial revolution. This may be true, but I think that as a result our systems and our processes were somewhat protected so that we could resurrect them in modern times. Now we have an opportunity to develop management systems that are optimal for our people and our place. Today, even mainstream postindustrial society is questioning the use of hierarchic, bureaucratic structures. We have been able to develop an alternative system that is derived from our own traditions and thought processes and have adapted it to our current needs. Like Japanese management techniques or the European quality circles, our system may have some general advantages over bureaucratic approaches; it certainly fits better with our specific communities.

I will conclude by saying that we had to gather information about and analyze the content and process of a whole range of traditional practices. Then we could start looking at parallels to Western systems and practices to figure out how to bring our cultural content from the 1700s and 1800s into the 20th and 21st centuries. By developing modernized processes and tools rooted in our own culture but matched to Western concepts and goals, we have been able to both promote internal community health and make possible true partnerships between our community and mainstream Western society. In the past, those who respected our traditions found themselves left out of the decision-making process. Now they can be confident that traditional roles and processes are helping to meet the contemporary goals and objectives of an energized Blackfoot people who look to the future with confidence.

George Thomas

22. The Value of Scientific and Engineering Training for Indian Communities

One of my former bosses, who was fairly excitable, came to me one day and said, "George, the time for action is passed. It is time for us to start talking about some of these issues." I hope he was not being prophetic about the theme of this book when he said that.

We have been going through some troubling times at the Cherokee Nation of Oklahoma, and I view those troubles as growing pains. If we want to achieve something, to improve the status of our many Indian nations, we are going to have to work our way through a lot of problems that will come our way.

I have tried to help solve those problems, and my professional background has contributed to my efforts. I am an engineer by training, but most of my career has not been in the engineering profession. Just the same, I use the experience that I gained in my training as an engineer on a day-to-day basis. I went into engineering for two primary reasons. First, I wanted to get a better understanding of how the physical world works, and second, I wanted to build something. From the reading that I had done as a young man, I felt that engineering was an outstanding discipline in which to pursue those two goals.

A number of the things that I have done through the years have been a direct result of my engineering training. I was instrumental in putting the American Indian Science and Engineering Society (AISES) together. I can remember initially contacting about 30 American Indian engineers about AISES. Things certainly have changed since then; at the end of 1996 I went to the AISES national conference in Utah and looked out into the hall during the keynote speech to see about 3,000 people. Today, when I travel around the country, it is not unusual at all to run into young Indian people who say that they anticipate studying science, engineering, medicine, and many other professions. A few years ago, that was almost unheard of. You would almost have to bend their arms to even get them to seriously consider engineering much less actually pursue it successfully at one of the top engineering schools around the nation, as many of our people do now. So it has been very rewarding to be involved with helping develop AISES through the years.

Engineering is, to me, a problem-solving discipline, which I have found to be of great value through the years. The other part of my engineering background that I use all of the time is its systems approach. In engineering, you are taught that everything is a system, and you learn how to analyze and work with those systems. To understand what I mean by "system," think about a person. A person has a number of processes—the cardiovascular, the skeletal, the muscular, the reproductive, the digestive, the nervous—that work, hopefully, in balance and in combination as an integrated system to maintain life, health, and the ability to act in the world. Our brain controls all of these systems, puts them all together, and hopefully makes them function correctly so that we have a well-balanced person. Now, consider a physician trying to diagnose the cause of an illness or a mechanic examining an engine that is out of tune. Both have to understand how the parts work together and how symptoms of poor functioning indicate problems with a certain part or with the connections between some parts. That is a systems approach. As an engineer, I like to see the balance, the integrated effective system, in everything that I am a part of; if it is not there, I use the systems analysis approach and the problem-solving skills I learned to try to figure out the source of the problem.

Not surprisingly, I have noticed that our Cherokee Nation is a collection of systems. The systems we have are numerous: accounting, purchasing, human resources, and program management, among others. Our tribal government is the brain. We have been in crisis because the systems (branches) of government are out of balance. I think that a lot of tribes, from what I have seen, have experienced similar problems. As a tribal government, we would like to over time be able to put that collection of systems into balance so that they all complement each other and all work in harmony. When we do that, we will be able to maximize the service that we are able to provide to our community, and the people who depend on us to be good stewards of the funds that come into the tribe will see that things are being done right.

The Cherokee Nation has experienced a tremendous period of growth over the last few years. During the last 20 years, the amount of money coming into the tribe has grown immensely. We have gone from very few employees, around 25 or 30, up to the point now where we have about 1,800. Many of the systems that we had in place were never changed as the government, and the number of employees and the type and number of services we provide, grew and evolved.

One thing that happens in a period of rapid growth, particularly when you are not paying careful attention to the development of your systems, is that you tend to develop a tremendous amount of inefficiency. We currently have that situation in the Cherokee government and, I believe, in many other tribal governments. Many of the problems come from segmenting services. Now with our managers we are looking at how we might integrate all of these programs to get people to think of themselves as a part of the Cherokee Nation and to work together to achieve important goals rather than just thinking of themselves as a separate unit within the tribal structure. With 1,800 people in a system that has been in place for 20 years, a tremendous amount of inertia has been built into the system. ("Inertia" is another engineering word that I thought I would throw in to prove I really am an engineer.) We have to overcome that inertia in our tribal structure and system so that they can handle our changing circumstances.

When I look at the Cherokee Nation, I see that it is part of a much grander system. I believe that the Cherokee Nation in and of itself will have a difficult time if we do not coordinate with other tribes from around the country. One of the things that disturbs me as I look across Indian country is that we do not have, in my view, a set institution, a structure with other tribes that builds toward something that we can truly call Native America. The Cherokee Nation and, I believe, other Indian nations need to build systems among themselves; they need to build the kinds of tools that are necessary to help us support the growth we are experiencing and to support the changes that many of us would like to see in the future. We need somehow to be both independent and part of a unified whole of Native people.

Many tribes spend a lot of time looking at their goals and objectives for the next 20, 50, or 100 years. Certainly we do this in the Cherokee Nation. Then we look at our goals in the framework of our government and determine how we are going to try to achieve them. But it is very difficult for us to achieve those goals and objectives without levels of institutional, economic, infrastructure, and skill support that are largely nonexistent at the moment. We cannot expect any substantial help from mainstream society to create them any time soon.

The Cherokee Nation in Oklahoma is the second-largest tribe in the United States. We have a membership of 180,000, of which about 110,000 live in Oklahoma. Our total financial impact is on the order of 1 billion dollars, which translates into several thousand jobs. Yet, despite the size of our membership and our billion dollar economic impact, we still do not have the human, technological, or economic ability to engineer the institutions or processes needed to educate our children, preserve and strengthen our culture, or fully provide for the needs of our people. Can any other Indian nations, almost all of which have fewer human and economic resources than does the Cherokee Nation, manage alone if the Cherokee Nation cannot? I do not believe so. Therefore, we need to cooperate among Indian nations to create the needed institutions and systems for ourselves. We need to have in place banking institutions, educational institutions, grass-roots organizations, economic exchange networks, and a lot of other systems to connect us all and help us work together toward good health and effective functioning. It is just like that brain I was talking about, which runs the body that brings all these systems into balance. We need to have something out there that will help us pull together our goals and collect and build the tools necessary to meet our needs. We need to bring Native America together to make our resources and strengths work together for the success of us all. I think this vision fits in with the idea that Keith James is working on: trying to bring us all together to begin to think about and to develop some collaborative strategies and common goals that will assist, not hinder, individual tribal goals.

What, you might ask, can we as a collection of over 500 tribes do to build something that will both aid our individual goals and build a real Native America? I have a couple of suggestions to offer. One was a major part of the theme of the conference from which this book comes: education. One thing that really motivated me early on and when we were thinking about AISES was the fact that Indian communities need engineering skills but do not have a large pool of Indian engineers from which to draw. We knew that if we were going to get more of the kinds of skills needed in Indian communities, then we were going to have to increase the overall pool of Native American engineers, scientists, and others. I thought that it was extremely important to increase the number of Indian graduates of, especially, science and engineering programs. We succeed at that, but it still did not quite work out as we had hoped.

What I have seen in the Cherokee Nation, and in many others, is that we are spending a tremendous amount of our limited resources on the education of our young people, but at the same time we are losing a lot of the ones who graduate to jobs elsewhere. We devote many dollars to scholarship money and to various other kinds of education programs to help get them educated as engineers, lawyers, doctors, and so on; but then they go out into the greater community and greater society, and we get very few of those young people back to help serve and build our community. I think that part of the reason for this is that our educational system is not necessarily appropriate to our needs.

Colorado State University was the setting for the conference upon which this book is based; like all mainstream educational institutions, it is in the business of educating young people to go out and find worthwhile jobs in the society of the United States at large. When our Indian students come to institutions such as this, they do not get any encouragement to go back into the Indian community, where they are desperately needed. To the contrary, they are encouraged to work for mainstream institutions and organizations, which receive assistance with recruiting them. I would like us to consider our own higher educational systems using our models and targeted to our needs to help us develop our people, which are our greatest resources as Indian communities and as Indian nations.

Control of our own educational systems at all levels is crucial to building tribal and intertribal unity, goals, resources, and systems that will benefit all of us. I think back to a book I read many years ago on the development of the Jewish homeland in Israel. I think it was David Ben-Gurion who walked across Israel, and when he emerged on the other side he concluded that two main things were crucial to the rebuilding of their nation. One of them was the need to speak a common language. I think that, in general, Indian people do this across tribes; the language is English. The other thing he concluded was the need for strong educational institutions throughout the country. If we continue to rely on an educational system that is not appropriate to our needs, our individual nations may not survive, and we could never build a greater Native American nation. How do we bring the best minds within the Indian community together to help young Indian people develop the necessary knowledge to help us push the envelope and develop businesses, our resources, and our governmental infrastructures? This is necessary if we are to survive and succeed as individual tribes. It is also necessary if we are to build something greater from all of the various tribes around the country working together.

Here is another example of an area where we need to work together across tribal boundaries. One of the resources we have as Indian nations is that we do not pay state or federal taxes on the enterprises the tribe develops. We

Cherokees, as a nation, have agreed not to tax the activities of the state of Oklahoma or the U.S. federal government as long as they do not tax ours. But a congressman drafted a piece of legislation that says that any income generated using land we take into trust from now on would be subject to federal and state taxes. This would put an end to any land acquisitions by the tribe because they would threaten our independence as a nation. While the proposed legislation did not get enough votes to become law, efforts to pass it continue. These are the kinds of pressures being placed on Indian tribes throughout the country by mainstream society that we need to work together to resist and address.

Colorado State University, the site of the conference mentioned above, is located in Fort Collins. At one point during the western expansion, a fort was actually built to try to protect the western settlement of non-Indians. We can use that image as a metaphor to say that we as tribes need to build forts to defend our efforts to go beyond the barriers of stereotypes and mainstream pressures and hindrances so that we can expand our health and strength. We have not had the educated young people or the tribal leadership to step forward and build our own Fort Collins on the leading edge of our journeys and to shore up and protect our next venture forward. This is what I mean when I talk about the need for institutions and organizations that can help us move ahead. This progress takes systems, it takes people who have a common vision, and it takes people who are dedicated not only to talking about these things but to doing whatever it takes to bring that vision into reality.

Engineering, to me, is a building profession. It is a building discipline. I think we need to continue to try to get more Indian young people involved in it, but just training more of our people to be engineers is not enough. Engineering needs to be integrated into some whole, into a unifying vision, into systems of systems that will build individual Indian nations and the nation of Native America.

Returning to what my former boss once said, I hope that the time for action has not passed. I do not think that it is too late for us. I believe that our time is just coming, because I believe that what we have gone through in the past has helped us grow, and I know that we have people who are now building the institutions that I consider to be critical for our path into the future. I hope I live to see large numbers of Indian young people taking up the tools of the builder and creating strong communities and a strong Native America. Contributing to that vision for my Cherokee community in Oklahoma as well as for Indian communities across North America would be legacy enough for me.

Cliff Atleo

23. Land, Science, and Indigenous Science

Tales from a Modern Treaty Negotiation Process

Let me start by saying that I feel very lucky and proud these days, because I am helping to realize the dreams of my ancestors. We have drawn the Canadian federal government and the British Columbian provincial government into negotiating a new relationship with our First Nations governments. I am proud of that, and you will understand why when I give you the background of how we became involved in a modern-day treaty-making process.

In general there are no treaties in British Columbia. Only the northeastern corner of the province and a couple of small areas on Vancouver Island are covered by any treaty; these are very small parts of a huge province. Our lands were simply declared crown land without regard to the Native people who had lived on them and cared for them for eons. Over 95% of the province was simply appropriated unilaterally in that way. In our view, the provincial and federal governments have stolen our land.

The first delegation of chiefs to go to England to discuss our lands was from Nis'ga in 1887. A second delegation went over in 1907 from the Squamish Nation. Other delegations of chiefs attempted to meet with the Royal Governor in Victoria in the early part of the 20th century, but they were turned away unheard. In 1927 a law was passed in British Columbia saying that the First Nations of the province had no further land rights and that the province would no longer discuss land issues with us. It became illegal for Native people to organize to even try to get land rights. The general goal in British Columbia and all of Canada at the time was to force Indian people to completely assimilate into white society.

In 1930 an organization called the Native Brotherhood of British Columbia was founded and patterned after the Native Brotherhood of Alaska, which had already been functioning for about 16 years. In 1930 one of the chiefs from Haida went up to the Native Brotherhood of Alaska annual meeting and came back with the idea of starting a similar organization in British Columbia. Since it was illegal to meet to discuss the land question, the participants sang "Onward Christian Soldiers" at the founding meeting of the Native Brotherhood of British Columbia so that it would qualify as a religious meeting in the eyes of the provincial police. So to this day the organization opens every meeting by singing "Onward Christian Soldiers." It was through the Native Brotherhood of British Columbia that the land question was kept open during the years when the government tried to make the asking of it a crime.

The government was finally forced to change its policy of abolishing land rights and even of abolishing the right of the people to question that policy when the Nis'ga challenged them once again. A Nis'ga leader named Frank Calder took the case of their land rights all the way to the Supreme Court of Canada. They lost by one vote on a technicality, which was that a federal law required the tribe to request and receive permission to sue before filing its suit. Since they had not done so, it was decided that the suit could be dismissed, regardless of its merits. Because the provincial and federal governments had come so close to losing that suit, the federal prime minister of the day, Pierre Trudeau, decided that he had no choice but to throw out the old British Columbian land policy along with the federal White Paper policy of attempting to force the assimilation of First Nations people. Trudeau opted for genuine negotiations with our people.

The provincial government at that time was not at all friendly to First Nations people, but they gave in to federal pressure and agreed to a three-way negotiation process to try to develop a modern, made-in-British Columbia treaty. Since we viewed the provincial and federal actions of taking our lands as illegal, we felt we were giving up something simply by coming to the negotiating table. We agreed to share the land by agreeing to negotiate, and our people understand that. We are granting the white governments a right to have a say about our lands by agreeing to negotiate the land issue with them from a position of equality. We formed what we call the British Columbia Summit of Chiefs, an organization of all of the hereditary chiefs of all of the Native groups in British Columbia, and in 1992 they successfully negotiated a 19-point agreement with the federal and provincial governments on procedures for the treaty-making process.

Point number 16 calls for the establishment of interim measures for shared management of resources on the lands that will be subject to treaty negotiation by First Nations governments and the provincial and federal governments. This point was included to recognize the need for ways of handling resource issues while the treaty negotiations were under way. It was clear that resource exploitation was going to move more quickly than the pace of treaty negotiations. So provision 16 was needed to accommodate ongoing commerce, business, and industry. It also gave First Nations people a say in their own lands and resources rather than, as had been the case for the 100 or so previous years, giving control of them almost entirely over to the white governments.

Although the provincial and federal governments had agreed to establish procedures for interim joint resource control, they did not live up to that part of their promise. They continued to deal with natural resources largely the way they always had. For instance, in 1993 they announced a plan to log a part of the Clayoquot Sound watershed without consulting with the Native people of the area. My tribe is situated in the heart of the Clayoquot Sound area. The tribal council, which is made up of 14 tribes, 13 of which are involved in treaty negotiations, has three regions: north, central, and southern. My tribe is one of five in the central region that work together very closely. Three of the five have traditional territories that cover the Clayoquot Sound watershed. Three or four months before the logging plan was publicly announced, our hereditary chiefs went to meet with the premier of the provincial government and his minister of Aboriginal affairs and told them that they could not simply make a decision by themselves about logging in the region. The officials tried to ignore the chiefs.

We were not going to be ignored, so we developed a strategy that included forming alliances with environmentalists, especially the Environmental Defense Fund. They told us about the success the Cree Nation had experienced in lobbying officials in New York State to refuse to enter agreements to buy power from the Province of Quebec. Quebec had wanted to build the James Bay hydroelectric project on land that they planned to expropriate from the Cree over Cree objections. Some powerful parties helped the Cree Nation, including the Environmental Defense Fund, Robert Kennedy Jr., and the family of then Governor Cuomo of New York. We decided that we should follow a similar approach.

We went, with environmentalist allies, to lobby at the United Nations headquarters and to meet with members of the U.S. government, including President Clinton, to try to get them to support us by putting pressure on the British Columbian and Canadian federal governments to live up to the agreement for shared interim decision making on natural resources. At the same time, we kept the media back in British Columbia informed of what we were doing and why. We told them that we had an agreement specifying joint interim decision making and that the province was violating the agreement and in doing so, our human rights.

We used other strategies to pressure the government as well. For instance, there is an island called Meer's Island in English that my people share equally with our neighbors, the Clayoquot First Nation. The provincial government approved logging there, too, without our agreement. So we went to court and got an injunction to stop the logging. We did this by demonstrating our historic rights to the island and showing that the provision of the treaty-process agreement that called for shared interim decision making had been violated by the government.

Soon, the British Columbian premier called and said that he wanted to negotiate with us. He said, "We can meet wherever you like, I'll have my ministers fly in." Hawaii came to mind as a good location, but we met with them back in Victoria, the capital of British Columbia, instead. When we met with the premier and the minister of Aboriginal affairs, they brought with them the province's chief treaty negotiator.

We told the premier that we could and would extend the injunction for Meer's Island to include the entire Clayoquot Sound region if they did not agree to put into immediate effect the provision of the treaty-process agreement that called for interim joint decision making. We even had all the figures laid out pertaining to litigation costs and our plan for financing it. We told the premier that his only options were either to put joint decision making into effect or to litigate, in which case we would shut down the entire economy of the area. He had his chief negotiator sit down with us that day to start working out the details for interim resource decision making. We ended up with something that actually gives us power.

We looked at all of the policies and all of the laws regarding resources on crown lands and found that not one of them considered First Nations' interests or values, not one. So we had to create a mechanism that would do so. We created a board called the Clayoquot Sound Regional Planning Board. It is designed to work by consensus, but it is also designed to give us real power through a veto. The board has five First Nations representatives, whom we select, and five non-Native representatives, who are chosen by the provincial government. The governing principles of that board include a clause that says that no decision can be made by the board without a double majority. That is, both a majority of the First Nations representatives and a majority of the members of the full board have to endorse a project or plan for it to be approved. We felt very strongly that there are principles to which both sides could agree and that the mechanism of a double majority would force the board members to find and operate by those shared principles. The government did not like the term "veto power," but that is really what we have because, unless at least three of our representatives support a decision, it cannot go forward. We, on the other hand, only have to get one of the provincial representatives to vote with our five members, assuming for the moment that our representatives are in agreement with each other, for a decision to pass.

Now, if things do deadlock in the planning board, the province does still technically have the final say. An issue that the board cannot decide is supposed to go up to the provincial cabinet for consideration. But the agreement we reached requires that any issue the provincial cabinet is going to decide must be publicly debated between our chiefs and the cabinet ministers. We know the provincial government will never want to do that. We built in mechanisms like that to provide the maximum incentive for the planning board to find common ground. And it is working. The proof came recently when we had a period of incredible rain. A lot of rain is not unusual in that area, but this was much more than normal, and a number of landslides occurred as a result. A few of those slides were in old growth areas, but most were in places that had been recently logged and had some regrowth on them. Now, logging had already taken place in six areas our planning board had approved in the period between the founding of the board and the downpour. No slides occurred in those six areas, but many occurred in areas that had been approved for logging before the board was established. That says to me that the board is making the right choices.

Even while the negotiations for the establishment of the planning board were under way, the province established a scientific panel to make recommendations for managing the Clayoquot Sound region. They did this because there was international pressure, from Europe as well as from the United States, to address the environmental issues that we had raised. The province appointed a number of different types of environmental scientists to that panel. So we said to the provincial government, "We like your idea for this panel, but we don't like the fact that you are excluding our people." We told them we wanted our one person with a doctorate to be on the panel but, in addition, wanted those among us with the equivalent of a doctorate in traditional knowledge of the environment also to be members. They agreed, and the whole idea of consensus-based decision making that we had built into the planning board was adopted by the scientific advisory panel. It now has the same kind of double majority requirement for recommendations that is required of the planning board's decision making. We think that the scientific advisory panel is quite a milestone for a couple of reasons. First, it is the first time we got both the scientific community and the government to acknowledge and accept the value of our traditional knowledge. Second, the panel's first recommendation was to take an inventory of the resources throughout the area of the sound as the initial phase of the planning process. That is something we had been asking for from the beginning of the process of negotiating for the establishment of the planning board. We thought that that kind of information was really needed to serve as a basis for developing good plans for managing the resources of the region, and we were right. It turned out that the government had been basing a lot of its decisions on false information and false assumptions.

For instance, we had asked the government, "How do you determine how much logging is allowed annually within your plans?" They answered that they used data provided by the logging companies to decide how much harvesting could be done in each area. We asked for an audit of the companies' figures. Audits were done in six regions, and it turned out that there was excessive cutting in every single one. Between 17 and 34% more cutting was being done in each audit area than was environmentally sound. The logging companies were giving the government false figures, and since the government was basing its decisions only on those figures, the companies were getting permission to cut much more than they should have been. They were getting away with murder.

How can you manage anything if you do not know what you have? I am not a forester, but it only makes sense to me that to manage a forest you have to know what is growing in each part of it before you can harvest anything. It always boggles my mind that the government and the logging companies will not recognize that you cannot just continue to try to increase the harvest every year to increase profits. The resources are not infinite, and if you keep increasing the take without regenerating the resources, eventually it will knock your profit line down to nothing. In our area, there was a projection a couple of years ago that if logging kept going at the existing rate, in 25 years there would be no old growth at all. We think that there should always be old growth. How? You find out the rate at which trees and forest areas develop, and you keep your harvest at a rate that allows for the development of old growth areas to replace the ones you are cutting. If you do not cut any more than that, then you will have old growth forever. We also need to know how the cutting in a certain area might affect other things under discussion in the treaty process, such as medicinal plants, salmon streams, or culturally important areas. You see, when we fought for our interim measures planning agreement, we never opposed logging. We believe that resources are there for our benefit. But they are not there for our abuse; we have to take care of them. That was not how the government had been operating up until then, though. So we made sure that the agreement for the planning board dealt with the issue of the status of the regional resources.

Another benefit of the planning board is that it has forced the different government ministries to talk to each other. There is the Ministry of the Environment, the Ministry of Forestry, and the Ministry of Aboriginal Affairs, and they have tended to operate as if their areas do not affect each other. Mainstream society is good at partitioning things off into boxes, whether they are truly distinct or not. The three ministries I just listed generally do not know what the others are up to, even though decisions that one ministry makes often have an impact on the issues that the others are supposed to be managing. But we have shown them that their areas and actions *do* intersect and have made those ministries wake up and begin to realize that they need to communicate and try to coordinate with each other. This fight against division and cubbyholing is a place where First Nations people can be a catalyst in promoting a more holistic view to counter the tendency to focus only on immediate financial gain.

In addition to the approaches to changing the planning process and managing the environment that I have already mentioned, we tried to learn from the innovations of other Native groups. Some of the most sophisticated forest resource management in the world is being practiced by Indian groups in the United States. For example, the Menominees of Wisconsin have done some wonderful things, and the Yakimas in Washington State have developed some resource management practices that are far better than what is being done anywhere else in the world. The Yakimas, for instance, are the leaders in understanding the spotted owl, which has sparked so much recent controversy in the United States. They have sent people out to study those owls for years, and they were the first to learn that each bird needs an area of 75 undisturbed acres. Our people have come down south to look at what such groups have done and have tried to adapt it to the Clayoquot Sound region.

I always make my environmentalist friends back home a little nervous by saying that I do not like parks. I do not like parks because they are intended to protect the land from people. What does that say about us? It says that we cannot manage the land to promote biodiversity while also meeting our needs—that, in effect, we cannot manage ourselves. We believe that people have a role to play in "natural" places. People are a part of nature, and without them as integral parts of places rather than as brief visitors, environments are diminished in health and wholeness. So we say, "Of course we can live in harmony with wild lands. Our ancestors did."

The sad thing is that ours is still the only area where provision 16 of the treaty-process agreement has been put into effect. The province has said that they are not interested in using the Clayoquot Sound planning board as a model for other areas. Unfortunately, none of the tribes in other parts of the province have been able to duplicate the kind of pressure we put on the government to develop the planning board with us. No group of tribes in an area has been able to cooperate closely enough with each other to put pressure on the provincial government, nor have they been able to build the kind of coalitions with outside groups that would help with that.

As a way of concluding, let me return to the larger treaty-making process out of which the Clayoquot Sound Regional Planning Board developed. I think this effort at modern-day treaty making is very interesting and may provide some models—such as our shared decision-making resource planning board—that could be useful to other indigenous groups around North America and around the world

All Native groups in North America were whole, complete societies before contact. We had astronomers, we had engineers. Did you ever see the long houses on the West Coast? They were built from huge logs and stood 10 or 15 feet off the ground. Engineers did that. We had doctors, medicine, navigators, and spiritual leaders. Our quest is to pursue that wholeness again. To regain our health, to understand our environment, to know how to take care of it, and to know how to get it to take care of us—that is what we seek. Our people were once whole, healthy, self-governing, and self-sustaining. If our ancestors could do that, so can we. We have to believe that, despite all of the negatives voices that often crop up. I like Frank Dukepoo's message of "I will never give up." I am also excited about some of the other ideas presented by the other authors in this book. I came away from the conference upon which these chapters are based with a lot of fresh ideas to take back to my people and to use in our efforts to negotiate a treaty.

We are all trying to find the best way to educate our children in Western skills while not losing our past, our history, and our roots that are so deep in the soil of North America. I believe that there is a way to do that, and we as a people will find a way to have the best of both worlds. We cannot afford to continue down the path that we have been on for these many recent decades. White society cannot afford it either. Throughout this book, statistics and cases document the relatively poor health, the economic and educational difficulties, and the other problems that we as Indian people currently face. We need to find ways to address those problems and to inspire our youth to help. Keith, Frank, and many others have offered ideas in their chapters for doing those things. I like those ideas and suggest that we continue to work together to make them succeed in the future. In my area, we have 14 tribes, but we work together as one. If you look at federal funding for Native people across Canada, you will find that it is higher in British Columbia than in any other part of the country. That is because we work together as one, through the British Columbia Summit of Chiefs, across the province on funding issues. Just so, perhaps Native people across North America can work together as one to begin to collectively influence the seemingly intractable people and circumstances that keep us entrenched in problems.

I say to you that we have a lot of problems, but we also have a lot of ideas and a lot of possibilities. We can manage, and we will.

Keith James

Conclusions

Closing the Circuit

One reviewer who commented on draft versions of the chapters in this volume expressed a pessimistic view of the situation and prospects in Indian communities. I do not agree with that assessment.

Clearly, Indian communities and Indian individuals have faced and continue to face substantial problems. It is certainly true that Indian history contains many painful events that still affect current circumstances. Some of the attitudes of mainstream North American societies toward Indian peoples have evolved, as have some of the attitudes and values of mainstream science. But those societies—their attitudes and the structures and systems they set up to deal with and control Native people—are still rooted in the condescension and hostility of yesteryear. Similarly, many of the attitudes, strategies, and values of science are rooted in the systems and structures of Western societies or in tendencies that were once useful or tolerable but whose time seems to have passed. Unless some of those systems, structures, strategies, and attitudes are uprooted and replaced, the Indian present and future will continue to be infected by the plagues of the past.

Yet some of us have come through safely. Despite the best and worst efforts to stamp out tribal cultures, the core of many cultures survived, and many tribes have begun to strengthen and expand again. There is a vibrancy and energy in the new generations of Indian peoples, and many exciting initiatives are under way that hold great promise of producing substantial benefits. The decline of tribes occurred rapidly, and their reascension might, as various tribal prophecies indicate, also be sudden. The authors in this volume, the collaborators in their projects, and the many other Native builders they represent are working, step by step, to address Indian issues and achieve tribal goals. As Freda Porter-Locklear writes, they are helping this one where they can. One by one, a critical mass is being built that may flash over into rapid advance to haleness.

In conclusion, the core message of this book is that two extreme opinions present in society—that science has nothing of value to offer Indian people and that Indian cultures have nothing of value to offer science—are, though held by different groups, both wrong.

Tradition does not stay stable; rather, it evolves, and Indian life has always been a dynamic exchange. It involves adaptation, but it always has a core or thread through it that links it together with what is fundamentally sound and true.

Mainstream institutions often communicate to Indian students and communities, in both verbal and nonverbal ways, the following sentiments: "You've got to adapt, you've got to become modern, you've got to move into mainstream educational institutions and mainstream science and mainstream society and forget the past and forget your history and traditions. They only hold you back." My response would be, "There may be a bit of truth to what you say, but it is vastly incomplete. The institutions and people of mainstream United States and Canada need to adapt to Indian people, too. In the long run, your institutions need Indian people and Native perspectives, as well, maybe more than Indian people need mainstream institutions, knowledge, or perspectives. Science, education, and mainstream society need some Indian ways and some Indian perspectives to help deal with the problems they have created and to help make additional advances. It needs to be a two-way dance."

The authors in this volume have charted some of the music and steps of the dance for us. They are a tremendously talented group who have all been successful in their own work and who have all been very dedicated to serving their communities. For that dedication and for the time they gave to the conference, to this book, and to future projects and plans, I thank and praise them. Ya:wˆ, my friends, ya:wˆ, n'iu.

Contributors

Joseph S. Anderson is an associate professor in the Management Department at Northern Arizona University.

Cliff Atleo (Nuu-chah-nulth First Nation, British Columbia) is one of the founders of the Clayoquot Sound Regional Planning Board.

Reggie Crowshoe (Blackfoot) is the director of Keeping Our Circle Strong Cultural Renewal Project for the Peigan Nation in Alberta.

Frank Dukepoo (Hopi) was an associate professor in the Department of Genetics at Northern Arizona University.

Lillian Dyck (Cree) is a professor in the Neuropsychiatry Research Unit at the University of Saskatchewan.

Jhon Goes in Center (Oglala Lakota) is the president of Innovative Geographic Information Systems, Inc.

Keith James (Onondaga/Minsi Lenape) is an associate professor of organizational psychology in the Department of Psychology at Colorado State University.

Ron Jamieson (Mohawk) is the executive vice president of the Bank of Montreal.

Gilbert John (Navajo) is an assistant professor in the Department of Microbiology and Molecular Genetics at Oklahoma State University.

Oscar Kawageley (Yup'ik) is an associate professor of education at the School of Education, University of Alaska, Fairbanks.

James Lujan (Taos Pueblo) is the Dean of Instruction at Southwestern Indian Polytechnic Institute.

Jane Mt. Pleasant (Tuscarora) is an associate professor at Cornell University, where she teaches agronomy in the Crop and Soil Sciences Department and is the director of the American Indian Program.

Cornel Pewewardy (Comanche/Kiowa) is an assistant professor in the Department of Teaching and Leadership at the University of Kansas.

Clifton Poodry (Seneca) is a program officer at the National Institute of General Medical Sciences.

Freda Porter-Locklear (Lumbee) is a lecturer at Pembrooke State University and the University of North Carolina.

Gerri Shangreaux (Oglala Lakota) taught in the College of Nursing at the University of South Dakota. She is currently affiliated with Cook County Hospital and teaches at Malcolm X College in Chicago.

Dean Howard Smith (Mohawk) is an associate professor in the Economics Department at Northern Arizona University.

George Thomas (Cherokee) is a nuclear engineer with the American Indian Science and Engineering Society national office in Albuquerque and is the former chief of staff of the government of the Cherokee Nation of Oklahoma.

Ofelia Zepeda (Tohono O'odham) is a professor in the Department of Linguistics and the Department of American Indian Studies at the University of Arizona and is also the director of the American Indian Language Development Institute.

Index

DATE DUE

JUL 0 5 2002			
NOV 0 1 2002			
DEC 0 1 2003			
MAR 2 2 2004			
OCT 3 1 2005			

Demco, Inc. 38-293